FOND MEMORIES FROM THE FORGETTABLE DECADE

FOND MEMORIES FROM THE FORGETTABLE DECADE

A Sports Fan's Attempt to Rehabilitate the 1970s

JIM BELLANO

PALMETTO
PUBLISHING
Charleston, SC
www.PalmettoPublishing.com

Hardcover: 979-8-8229-3233-3
Paperback: 979-8-8229-3234-0
eBook: 979-8-8229-3235-7

*For
Jaclyn and Jenna*

CONTENTS

Introduction

It was the best of times; it was the most mediocre of times. It was the age of leisure suits; it was the age of disco jeans. It was the epoch of Led Zeppelin; it was the epoch of the Bee Gees. It was the season of runaway inflation; it was the season of malaise. It was the spring training of optimism; it was the winter of playoff elimination. Or, so Dickens may have said if he grew up in the 1970s. And, minus the guillotines.

At first blush, writing a book that celebrates life in the 1970s may seem like quite a stretch, an enormous undertaking requiring some heavy lifting indeed. However, if there is a bias in my presenting a theory that the 1970s was a great decade, I suspect it is mine and specifically personal. For me, a teenager navigating my formative years through the seventies, I am not pretending that in the history of mankind, or the world, or even the United States, that the seventies occupy some Mount Olympus of historical and cultural prominence in the hearts and minds of the American people. For me, however, it was a fabulous time.

This book is more eulogy than elegy. A requiem as opposed to a dirge. It is a celebration of an otherwise lamentable era. My family history and interactions with friends put forth in these pages are presented in order to better define and give the proper perspective for what is the ultimate thesis of this book—that my experiences as a sports fan from the era surpass those of any other fan from any other place and any other time. Buttressing this argument is the fact that from October of 1970 to January of 1980, my teams appeared in nine Major League Baseball (MLB) League championship series that resulted in four World Series rings and six National Football League (NFL) championship games that culminated in four Super Bowl victories.

To further the Dickensian analogy from above, this book is also a tale of two cities. It is a story of New York and Pittsburgh. The Big Apple and the Steel City. The City That Never Sleeps and the City of Champions. Gotham and the Burgh.

Again, let's be clear: a book lauding the 1970s is by no means a monumental claim. To some, it may seem trivial, perhaps even frivolous. However, it is not a spurious one either. Sports were everything to me in the 1970s. It was the sun around which my planet revolved.

Yes, the Forgettable Decade had no V-E Day or V-J Day and no marches on Washington, and the Dow never closed to a record high. For me, however, none of this matters.

Unlike '60s Baby Boomers who have beguiled themselves into believing that American history began with them—that stamping their feet, shouting catchy antiwar rhymes, and getting college finals canceled is somehow on par with breaking away from Great Britain and creating a new nation, fighting the Civil War and ending slavery, and braving the Great Depression while defeating fascism and winning World War II. Those of us that endured both the good and the bad of the seventies are under no such delusion.

Sure, the '70s gave us Watergate, stagflation, gas lines, and eight-track tapes. We draped ourselves in a color palette containing hues of avocado green and burnt orange that enveloped everything from carpet to ceiling—including the kitchen appliances. It was also the decade that spawned polyester leisure suits. This hideous ensemble would be worn over a flower-patterned, Quiana shirt, another piece of clothing made from cheesy, nylon fabric that masqueraded as acceptable attire. This re-pugnant piece of apparel, unlike others of its fashion ilk, never garnered enough support for a comeback. Like, say, tie-dyed T-shirts.

There were, in fact, a number of influences that impacted my life in the 1970s. For example, it would be foolish to deny that my parents and family did not shape my personal and moral principles in anything less than a significant way. This would have been the case in my early years, as most of a child's life is molded by his or her parents during this formative time.

However, once I was old enough to wander the neighborhood alone or with friends, say, age ten or so, the majority of time that made up my day-to-day schedule consisted of four activities: sleeping, school, being out with my friends, and playing sports. With the exception of winters, when children are forced to stay inside for lengthy periods of time, my homelife was reduced to a mere pit stop, a place where one to three meals could be consumed and a bed would be provided. In the end, therefore, I believe that parental and familial influence comes, for the most part, through osmosis.

From that point on, with the ability to leave the nest and with this foundation of personal and moral conventions firmly ingrained, friends then become most responsible for the next stage of youth devel-opment—social values. During these years, many friendships are made. Some become lifelong; others dissipate into the mist with the transition from elementary to high school. Having two older sisters as siblings, who were four and seven years older than me, respectively, and who went off to college while I was still in grade school and high school, it was my brothers from other mothers who provided the stone and chisel for sculpting my seventies experience. In addition to doing what teenagers do (i.e., hang out, drive around, and talk about nonsense), nowhere did I spend more time with my friends than on the playing field.

In the spring and summer, we played baseball. The various incarnations that baseball would take depended on the time of year and the circumstances under which we could play.

Obviously, there was organized baseball. In my case, this was under the auspices of the Henry S. Richards Little League. We also had some friends that were part of a neighboring league, the Hillcrest Lakers. Extending the season, there could be travel leagues where we would be combined with players from different teams to compete against various squads from around the city. After the Little League season, we would play baseball as best we could, whenever we could, getting extremely creative at times.

Given the obvious difficulties for finding eighteen people to play at a given time for a pickup game, we would have to improvise. When this was the case, and it usually was, we played on a half field. Here, a pitcher would take the mound and, depending on the amount of players available, one or two people in both the infield and the outfield positioned themselves only on one side of second base. Any ball hit to the open field was an automatic out.

The regular season and World Series took place in our backyards, sometimes with a wiffle ball, sometimes with a hardball. In my case, the fence that separated my backyard from Tody's Woods acted as both Yankee Stadium's short porch and death valley.

Sometimes we would take the game to the street with countless contests played with a Spaulding replacing the wiffle ball for maximum distance up the steep Candlewood Drive hill and with a manhole cover representing home plate. "Pops Up," as it was known, was played one-on-one using the fungo technique.

There was high school baseball, but only a friend who went to Catholic high school and I played the sport in an organized way after Little League. This, however, did not deter us from cooking up other ways to enjoy America's pastime. I cannot begin to count the number of two-on-two stickball games that were played against a wall with a painted box as a strike zone at either PS 28 or PS 32.

Even rainy days were not a deterrent. In such situations, Strat-O-Matic Baseball would be employed.

In the fall, and as late into the winter as allowable, we played football—again, in an organized league like Henry S. Richards. Many friends went on to play in high school. But the majority of my gang did not. We played football anywhere and everywhere. At the aforementioned public schools, Andus Field, my friend Willie's backyard, and our favorite concrete venue, the Pembrooke Drive dead end. These were the days before the cul-de-sac was invented and children played without benefit of parental SUV or minivan escort.

When a full cadre of friends was around, a game of "touch" could turn into a classic battle. But four or six players worked just fine. If the number was even more limited and only an odd number of players were available, one player, sometimes an older brother, could be commandeered to act as "official quarterback," throwing down and outs, slants, and posts to both teams.

You would think football would be a nonstarter with only two players, but we were not deterred in these instances either. If necessary, on rare occasions, the imaginative adolescents hell-bent on playing would engage in one-on-one games featuring the "angel pass," a toss thrown to oneself in order to march downfield toward an opponent's end zone. Say what you will about the quality of play; we were nothing but creative.

There were only two things that could disrupt any of these epic contests. One, a maternal call from the home that dinner was ready. Sometimes it took two or three of these for play to be suspended. Some mothers used a cowbell in place of a yell. The second was the clanging of the Good Humor truck. The chimes emanating from George, the Good Humor man's vehicle, were like a steam whistle at the end of shift at a manufacturing plant or the bell signaling that the school day was over. This was our version of the TV timeout.

Like baseball, in inclement weather, an alternative activity in the form of electric football took center stage.

I would be remiss not to add Catholic school as being a key influence on my Forgettable Decade existence. To clarify, I am not talking about the Catholic religion, the Catholic Church, or even the Bible. Rather, while attending Catholic school for nine years, five days a week, taking a daily religion class, and serving as an altar boy for three years, I had my fair share of exposure to nuns, priests, and the liturgy. As a result of attendance at Catholic school and the dissemination of the scriptures therein, the institution left a fairly significant imprint on a portion of my life during the Forgettable Decade. Like an archeologist of the ancient Middle East that spends years pouring over hieroglyphic papyruses and cuneiform tablets, despite rarely attending church anymore, I can, in large part, go to mass today and still participate with rote accuracy.

Turning back to the realm of seventies sports, in many ways it was a golden age, particularly for me. It was the decade of Yankees resurgence as World Series champions. It was the birth of Steeler Nation. It was the era where the Pirates, who had been comatose since their upset win over the Yankees in 1960, became perennial contenders for the pennant and bookended the decade with World Series wins.

In trumpeting the 1970s sports landscape, I am not trying to turn lead into gold here. This is not cultural alchemy. I would argue acolytes of the sixties and, to a lesser extent the eighties, have spent many years trying to do just that with their respective decenniums. But, being raised Catholic, I am familiar with the miracle of transubstantiation. Given that, I believe the much-maligned 1970s, in my perspective, deserve a second look.

The word "nostalgia," while, in the modern sense, evokes good memories, comes from a combination of the Greek words *nostos* (homecoming) and *algos* (pain). Life, and the reminisces thereof, is never all good or all bad. My goal in the pages that follow is to bring some long-deserving appreciation to what is generally perceived as an otherwise dreadful time. In the language of ABC's *Wide World of Sports,* my goal is to reveal to the reader both "the thrill of victory and the agony of defeat." It is my way of reconciling, or perhaps rationalizing, two dissonant principles: one, the '70s sucked; and two, my subjective interpretation that the 1970s was a great decade.

In addition, mention must be made in the way in which I relate my baseball and football experiences. Baseball was my game. I wanted to grow up and play for the New York Yankees. With the exception of a short dalliance with wanting to be an astronaut during the glory days of Apollo launches and landings, there was no other career path I wanted than to be in pinstripes. Professional baseball was a game in which we could readily experience in person. Treks to Yankee Stadium and, God help us, Shea Stadium were relatively commonplace. Therefore, many of the memorable experiences with regard to baseball took place *dal vivo e di persona.*

Football was different. The once-a-week contests, especially for a 1970s youth, were watched exclusively on TV. I did not know anyone that attended a professional football game in person, although, once, Mr. Floyd took me and his son, Joey, to an Army-VMI (Virginia Military Institute) game at West Point.

Despite the disparity in viewing locations, both sports provided commensurate emotional highs and lows. The difference was that at a baseball game, we could be a mob. Watching football alone or in a small group, we were more like the psychotics speaking to themselves on the streets of Manhattan. I'm talking about bond traders, not the homeless.

Finally, some of the events recounted in this book have just celebrated their fiftieth anniversary. Some will approach that milestone shortly, and still others will reach their golden year in the near future. And, while this book is limited to football and baseball, the truth was, we followed and played virtually every sport. Basketball, hockey, boxing, golf, tennis—you name it—they were all in our recreational repertoire. Our appetite for sports was voracious. But time and word count compels me to limit the discussion in the following pages to only the diamond and the gridiron. Memories of other sports will have to wait for another day.

Chapter One
When (or Who) Were the '70s?

It might be easier to write an overview of the Forgettable Decade, or, for that matter, any decade, if I simply recounted my experiences within a sequential time frame (i.e., January 1, 1970, through December 31, 1979). However, "decades" as we know them, as we remember them, do not adhere to a simple chronological calendar. There are cultural and historical events that occur in a particular decennium that transcend mere chronology. Therefore, in attempting to identify a clear beginning to the Forgettable Decade, we might find it instructive to look at what is perceived as a more "memorable" era, the 1960s, and see how those parameters might be drawn.

Many would argue that the sixties did not begin until November 22, 1963, with the assassination of John F. Kennedy (JFK) and the national disillusion that followed. Others might contend that the arrival of The Beatles in the US on February 4, 1964, and the ensuing *British Invasion* mark the onset of the counterculture decade. Still, others might posit that August 7, 1964, the day Congress passed the Gulf of Tonkin Resolution and further cemented our long involvement in Vietnam, best marks the birth of the era. In any event, clearly, prior to President JFK's assassination, the sixties, as we've come to know them, had not yet arrived. America was still in a 1950s mindset.

Bearing this out, as late as mid-September 1963, more than two months before Lee Harvey Oswald poked his Mannlicher-Carcano rifle out of the fifth story of the Texas School Book Depository; or some yet unknown individuals simultaneously aimed their rifles over the picket fence on the Grassy Knoll; or, in the case of Oliver Stone types, the Mafia, Central Intelligence Agency (CIA), Federal Bureau of Investigation (FBI), National Security Council (NSC), Lyndon B. Johnson (LBJ), right-wing Cubans, Joe Pesci, and Tommy Lee Jones conspired to assassinate Kennedy, the number one single, according to *Billboard* magazine's Hot 100 was "My Boyfriend's Back" by The Angels. This excerpt from the song evinces the 1950s tenor of the lyrics and does not evoke the language of sixties' refrains such as, "Hey, Hey, LBJ, how many kids did you kill today?"

My boyfriend's back and you're gonna be in trouble
Hey-la-day-la my boyfriend's back
You see him comin' better cut out on the double
Hey-la-day-la my boyfriend's back
You been spreading lies that I was untrue
Hey-la-day-la my boyfriend's back
So look out now 'cause he's comin' after you

I think it is fair to assume, however, by late 1964, post-assassination disillusion had settled into the country, at least by way of popular music, which, of course, is the barometer by which sixties Baby Boomers measure everything. By that time, the *Billboard* charts were no longer dominated by early rock and roll icons like Elvis or Chuck Berry or their more saccharin-laced progeny, artists such as the Beach Boys and the Four Seasons. The 1950s rockers and doo-whoppers gave way to the new sounds of Motown and the British Invasion. More evident, perhaps, was the banishment from the charts of sappy pop artists like Pat Boone and Perry Como. In fact, from the first week of February 1964 (the date of The Beatles' arrival in the US), until year's end, the weekly top spot on the *Billboard* charts was occupied only thirteen times by artists that were either vestiges from, or extensions of, the 1950s pop charts. In 1965, that number held constant for American artists, but those spots were now occupied by groups like The Byrds, whose sound had changed dramatically from their fifties counterparts. Also, 1964–1965 listeners were introduced to the sound of Motown and elevated that genre to the number one spot seventeen weeks between 1964 and 1965. In addition, this new, fresher sound coming out of Detroit from the Motown artists was a departure from both early African American idols like Chuck Berry, Fats Domino, and Little Richard, and soft-toned, mainstream groups like The Platters, The Drifters, and The Coasters. The balance of chart toppers during this period was filled by The Beatles and other British Invasion artists. In sum, during the one hundred weeks from when The Beatles arrived until the end of 1965, the number one *Billboard* slot was held by either a British Invasion band or a Motown group 71 percent of the time.

To try to bookend the argument more concisely, by September of 1965, a clear transition in the culture had occurred. By the time Barry McGuire's doom and gloom single, "Eve of Destruction," went to number one on the *Billboard* charts, white, mainstream American artists (Motown artists had already begun carving their own unique path) were expressing themselves in ways aimed more and more toward the counterculture.

Don't you understand what I'm trying to say?
Can't you feel the fears I'm feeling today?
If the button is pushed, there's no runnin' away
There'll be no one to save with the world in a grave

Take a look around you boy, it's bound to scare you, boy
And you tell me over and over and over again my friend
Ah, you don't believe we're on the eve of destruction

Or, to put it in 1950s vernacular, *Hey-la-day-la, we're all gonna die.*

Whether the line of demarcation occurred with the JFK assassination, The Beatles' arrival in America, or LBJ's Tonkin Gulf Resolution, somewhere between Dealey Plaza and Barry McGuire, the "sixties" had arrived.

So, what about the seventies? Targeting the date for the beginning of the "1970s" is similarly, if not more, difficult to pin down. Early Forgettable Decade events such as the first Earth Day, April 22, 1970, and the killing of four students and wounding of nine others at Kent State University by Ohio National Guard troops on May 4, 1970, occurred in the seventies, but have more of a 1960s flavor to them.

Maybe the break-in at the Watergate Hotel, June 17, 1972, is a more apropos date? The break-in was the kickoff to what President Gerald Ford called, at his swearing in on August 9, 1974, after the resignation of Richard M. Nixon, "our long national nightmare." Or, was it the first Middle East oil embargo, what then was referred to as the Arab oil embargo, that saw the average price of gas jump 32 percent from thirty-six cents per gallon in 1972 to what then was the astronomical sum of fifty-three cents per gallon in 1974? Perhaps it was the ostensible end of the Vietnam War in January 1973, or the subsequent evacuation of Saigon in 1975?

And, while the taking and killing of Israeli athletes at the 1972 Summer Olympics, the Munich Games; the bombing at Fraunces Tavern in New York City; and, here and there, the odd passenger airline being commandeered by extremists were pivotal events, for the most part, these were isolated instances. Terrorism, as we have come to know it, had not yet taken form. This strain of cancer would not start spreading in earnest until the 1979 Iran hostage crisis and would not fully metastasize for decades until September 11, 2001.

Therefore, while we might find it edifying to look at music trends as we did with the 1960s in order to identify a hard start date for the 1970s, using that metric proves more difficult. Because the Forgettable Decade went through so many melodious fits and starts, it becomes challenging to link a particular style of music to characterize the decade. Moving from the vestiges of folk to the development of heavy metal rock, to disco, to Southern rock, to punk rock, and finally, new wave music, this *mish mosh* and overlapping of musical genres make it somewhat untenable for purposes of marking the start of the decade. While the 1970s gave us a lot of iconic, memorable music, including Led Zeppelin, the greatest rock band that ever was (sorry, Beatles fans), unfortunately, the Forgettable Decade also certainly gave us more than our fair share of bad music. This racket descended upon the public's cochlea and was often interspersed among tragedies that befell some of the music industry's best and, one might say, in biblical proportions.

Understanding that it might not be used for any other viable purpose in life, I will attempt to provide an abstract of the 1970s musical landscape by putting my nine years of Catholic school acumen to work. Therefore, this cataloging might best be represented by a litany that reads like a '70s musical version of the "Generations of Adam" in Genesis 5:

1. And Vicki Lawrence begat "The Night the Lights Went Out in Georgia," and it was a *Billboard* Hot 100.
2. And Jim Croce lived thirty years: and he died.
3. And Cher begat "Half Breed" and Terry Jacks begat "Seasons in the Sun," and both went to number one.
4. And Cass Eliott lived thirty-four years: and she died.
5. And woe unto us, the Starland Vocal Band begat "Afternoon Delight" and it, too, climbed the *Billboard* charts.

6. And three from Lynyrd Skynyrd lived unto their late twenties: and they died.
7. And, RSO Records begat the soundtrack to *Saturday Night Fever*; and, like the plagues of yore brought forth upon Egypt, a great pestilence was released upon the people.
8. And Keith Moon lived thirty-two years: and he died.
9. And A Taste of Honey begat "Boogie Oogie Oogie," and we wept.
10. And Sid Vicious lived twenty-one years: and he died.

Maybe you'd have had to have gone to Catholic school to appreciate this, but, in any event, none of this is very instructive for pegging the opening date for the Forgettable Decade. I have to admit, I was not then, and I am not now, much of a music aficionado. Perhaps, then, this discussion of music has taken us down the wrong path. In fact, it may be that I have been asking the wrong question entirely.

Given the vagaries associated with both the societal events and musical genres of the era, perhaps, a more cogent question for determining the start of the Forgettable Decade is not "*When* were the 1970s?" but rather, "*Who* were the 1970s?"

I believe it is significant to note that those of us born after 1958 (I am a '61) are still considered part of the Baby Boom generation (1946–1964). However, for a number of reasons, and for many children of the seventies, this is a misnomer.

Jonathan Pontell, described with the moniker "author and social commentator," coined the term "Generation Jones" in 1999 to describe late Baby Boomers—that is, those children born in the period 1954–1964. The term "Jones," according to Pontell, evinces the fact that this cohort is resentful and has a yearning, or "jonesing," for the benefits and opportunities bestowed on older Boomers and, therefore, should not be lumped into the same category as their spoiled counterculture counterparts (my term, not Pontell's) because they did not have the same experiences as early Boomers (e.g., eligibility for the draft during the Vietnam War).

In a 2009 piece for a website called Facts and Arts, Pontell, a product of GenJones himself, ends his column, oddly, with the following Bommeresque flourish, "For Boomers, the legacy of the 1960s is ideology, but for Jonesers it is idealism. That spirit of the sixties is far from dead; its seeds were planted in us as children then, and are flowering now. We're not late Boomers; we are late bloomers."

However, in my opinion, Pontell and his devotees got a couple of things wrong. First, the demarcation line between Boomers and Jonesers is a bit too generous. Pontell is being over inclusive by incorporating the 1954–1957 cohort into the group. Someone born as late as 1957 would be entering their sixteenth year as the end of the school year approached in 1973 and just as US troops were formally withdrawn from Vietnam. With college deferments long gone, this left plenty of time for the '57s to at least experience a couple years of angst over whether or not they might be drafted in the near future. At least enough to have them mentally associate with the "Hell no, we won't go" Baby Boomer cohort. Meanwhile, with the authority of the US military to induct via the draft having expired in July of 1973, any males born between 1958 and 1964 were, at most, either about to enter their sophomore year of high school on the high end (the '58s) or on their way to fourth grade (the '64s). In other words, this group was never going, nor did they have a fear of being sent, to Southeast Asia.

Second, as the ethos of the Joneser generation has manifested itself in me and my friends (all that matters for purposes of this book), GenJonesers are not idealistic. They are skeptical, even cynical. We were certainly not, as Pontell described, big on optimism. At least not until the American electorate sent Jimmy Carter packing. While Boomers have deluded themselves into believing they changed the world, GenJonesers got stuck with the world rolling over them in the form of Watergate, inflation, the Iran hostage crisis, and Jimmy Carter's national malaise. Boomers, as William Hurt's character, Nick, in *The Big Chill,* the coming-of-age movie for Baby Boomers and perhaps the second-most nauseating feature film of all time behind *St. Elmo's Fire,* remarked, "No one had a cushier berth than we [Baby Boomers] did."

Boomers got to make love, do drugs, and listen to music while getting finals canceled under the pretense of "making a difference." Gen-Jonesers had to wait in line for gas on odd-even license plate days.

I've always felt that a good test, albeit highly unscientific, for establishing the Boomer/Joneser line of demarcation would be to ask these children of the '50s and early '60s two questions, both of which are associated with the year 1969.

First, what was the biggest event of 1969? A true Baby Boomer would likely say, "Woodstock." A GenJoneser would reply, "the Apollo moon landing." There still may be a few former "college Republicans for Nixon" types around that, at the time, would have chosen Teddy Kennedy's drowning of Mary Jo Kopechne at Chappaquiddick, but I doubt they would admit to it now.

The second question involves a battle of the buddy films. Which was the best picture of 1969, *Butch Cassidy and the Sundance Kid* or Oscar winner *Midnight Cowboy?* GenJonesers recognize the Redford-Newman dynamic as setting the standard by which all buddy movies, past and present, are judged. The George Roy Hill–directed flick should have won Best Picture that year, period.

Boomers, on the other hand, would go with the latter, an edgy movie chronicling the relationship of a dipshit, cowboy-clad drifter coming to the big city to make his mark, not on the Great White Way, but as a male prostitute in Times Square and who is befriended by a disabled hustler without access to health care and who ultimately dies of pneumonia. Plus, Boomers would say, "*Midnight Cowboy* was given an X rating.

Isn't that cool?" OK, Boomer. Basically, the discussion comes down to, "Who are those guys?" versus "I'm walkin' here!"

Getting back to the question at hand and start date for the 1970s, for the purposes of this book, however, there is really only one important determination involved here (i.e., the beginning of "My Seventies"). For me, my affection for the 1970s is neither cultural, nor socio-political. It was about sports, and hanging out with friends, and, of course, girls, the *triple crown* of male adolescent life. To be more accurate, and avoiding the futility of parsing through musical lyrics and seminal historical events, I can specifically pinpoint the alpha and omega of my Forgettable Decade.

In the end, and despite all my jabbering about musical genres and early and late Boomers, my seventies began on June 6, 1970, and ended on February 22, 1980.

Chapter 2
Anatomy of a '70s Sports Fan

Before fully delving into a recitation of why my personal account of being a teenage sports fan in the 1970s is of any interest to, well, anyone, and as I contend rivals the greatest single decade experienced by any sports fan, there are a number of important precepts of fandom that bear noting in order to put that claim into proper context.

First, it would be easy for the reader to infer that recounting my euphoria associated with rooting for teams like the Yankees—the greatest dynasty in Major League Baseball history—and the Steelers—arguably the most successful franchise in the National Football League's postmerger era—smacks of my engaging in the detestable art of front running. We all know the type. New England Patriots fans that jumped on the bandwagon during the Brady-Belichick era, have no idea who Sam "Bam" Cunningham was, and are clueless to the fact that Jim Plunkett once threw touchdown bombs to Randy Vataha at a place called Schaefer Stadium. Similar to these loathsome characters include New Yorkers that blow with the wind and utter that most vile of pronouncements, "I like both the Yankees and Mets."

Therefore, it is important, up front, to emphatically deny that my unabashed love for the Pirates, Yankees, and Steelers came about without any association to the contemptible practice of front running, bandwagon jumping, or being a Johnny-come-lately. The forthcoming chapters and their contents will bear this out.

As I will explain, my attachment to these teams began at the time when the Yankees were bad, the Pirates just began achieving a degree of success, and, while the Steelers were becoming competitive, the jury was clearly out on a franchise that had stunk up the gridiron for most of the previous forty years. Also, as the reader will see, there are specific genealogical connections to these franchises that I came to adore. It is nothing short of my DNA that explains my love of these teams. It should be added, that like my premature gray hair that was passed down through genes on my mother's side, it is an appropriate analogy to say that I have been genetically engineered to root, root, root for these home teams.

Second, in order to fully appreciate a "fan's greatest decade" discussion, it is additionally imperative to articulate the passions around which the fan-team allegiance is built and capture the true mindset of a fan. That is, the essence of what actually makes such sports devotees tick.

While the true origins of the word "fan" may be somewhat unclear, from Webster's to Wikipedia, it is generally accepted that the word "fan" is derived from a shortened version of the word "fanatic." According to *Merriam-Webster's Collegiate Dictionary*, etymologically, "fan" comes from the modern Latin *fanaticus*, meaning "insanely but divinely inspired." Fair enough.

There is an alternative to the fanatic etymology, claiming that the term is derived from the word "fancy," as in, "I fancy a good cup of tea," or something to that effect. However, the term "fancy" carries with it a connotation much less intense than what we typically think of as the fan experience. "I genuinely fancied the time in San Diego when Ken Norton broke Muhammad Ali's jaw," falls woefully short of expressing any kind of accurate sentiment.

Furthermore, using "fancy" to describe "fans" sounds too genteel, akin to some Victorian era adage stated while drinking tea with one's pinky extended, and has no place being attributed to what we tend to know as American sports fans. Anyone that has been to a Yankees–Red Sox game can attest to this.

The Merriam-Webster Thesaurus additionally lists twenty variants as synonyms for the word "fan": addict, aficionado, buff, bug, devotee, enthusiast, fanatic, fancier, fiend, fool, freak, habitué, head, hound, junkie, lover, maniac, maven, nut, and sucker.

With the exceptions of buff, bug, habitué, and, again, fancier, which are too delicate to describe what I would consider a real fan, this catalog just about nails it. Also, the term habitué better describes the *hoi polloi* that make recurring trips to Disneyland or Branson, Missouri, than it does the Cheeseheads that frequent Lambeau Field. I would have excluded the word "suckers" as well, but, then again, in our lifetimes we all have come across Detroit Lions, San Diego Padres, Phoenix Suns, and Buffalo Sabres fans.

The thesaurus goes on to list thirty-two additional words as being "related to fan." These include: groupie, admirer, amateur, collector, connoisseur, authority, expert, adherent, convert, cultist, disciple, follower, hanger-on, votary, advocate, apostle, backer, champion, evangelist, exponent, friend, patron, promoter, proponent, supporter, partisan, and zealot.

Again, this additional list falls short of the type of sports fan I am referring to in this book (i.e., me), by tossing in terms such as amateur, collector, dilettante, booster, rooter, well-wisher, and faddist within its inventory. These terms, too, are way too soft and subtle to describe the quintessential fan. I can, however, live with proponent, supporter, partisan, and zealot.

Within this vein of fanaticism, it is the obligation of every fan to love their teams and pray for the destruction of any franchise that stands in the way of their team's success. It is also appropriately fanatical and acceptable to hate one's own team at specific times before reopening one's heart to them again. For reference, see Atlanta Falcons fans after the fourth quarter of Super Bowl LI.

Third, being a true sports fan is a very complicated business, especially for teenage boys, who, in their formative years, tend to see things in black and white. These are the same hormonal-driven instincts that have them focusing, even obsessing, on a limited number of topics, like girls, movies, perhaps music and cars, and, of course, sports. The emotional panoply involving these topics, to a teenage guy in the 1970s, was always expressed in definitive terms of the love-hate relationship. For example:

"Boston's second album sucks!"

"Rocky is the best movie ever!"

"Cathy Delmonaco is wearing a tube top today!"

Or, one of my favorites, while cruising up Central Avenue in Yonkers, one friend observed and commented on what a piece a shit a passing, beat-up Ford Mustang looked like. As a self-proclaimed muscle car devotee, Tommy O'Brien angrily turned around and shot back, "Fuck you! It's a Shelby!"

For me, in these formative years, when it came to the subject of sports, there was some but little room for gray area. As a guide to the remainder of this book, let me attempt to explain my approach to being a fan in the Forgettable Decade. It is best to use pro football for purposes of an example. To do a more comprehensive breakdown, sport by sport, league by league, would likely take up the balance of the book.

The most concise categorization that best summarizes my attitudes and passions toward National Football League teams in the Forgettable Decade can be recited as follows:

Team I loved: Steelers.

Teams I kind of liked: Jets, Browns, Oilers, Chiefs, Patriots, Packers.

Teams I didn't give a shit about: Bills, Chargers, Bengals, Broncos, Giants, Eagles, Cardinals, Rams, Redskins, Lions, Bears, Falcons, 49ers, and Saints (add the Buccaneers and the Seahawks beginning in 1976).

Teams I hated: Vikings, Colts, Dolphins.

Teams I fucking hated: Cowboys, Raiders.

To most accurately represent the essence of my '70s fandom, it is of paramount importance to note that the above system of classification, while static for the most part, could be subject to temporary fluidity. For example, while the category of "Teams I fucking hated" has remained constant, etched in marble over time, the other categories might, on occasion, shape-shift depending on the situation. As an illustration, pivoting to a quick baseball reference, see the 1975 and 1986 World Series. Being a despiser of all things Cincinnati Reds and New York Mets, I found myself in the unenviable position of being forced to root for, God forgive me, the Boston Red Sox, a team, with the exception of those two instances, I thoroughly loathe. In those respective fall classics, the Red Sox, never failing to crush the hopes and dreams of their own fans during those days, lost both World Series contests.

Shifting back to football, on any given Sunday, if a team I didn't give a shit about was playing a team I fucking hated, such a benign squad could be elevated to a team that I kind of liked. More rarely, even a game involving a team I hated, if it had playoff implications that benefitted the Steelers, could hoist even a detestable franchise into the "Teams I kind of liked" category, albeit only for three hours, give or take.

Fourth, it must be noted that fandom is not necessarily frozen in time. While, as mentioned, certainly the feelings for the team that I love and the teams that I fucking hate have remained fixed, sports, like the cosmos, have some perpetual consistency while constantly expanding on some level as well.

Therefore, the above hierarchy of love and hate is merely a snapshot of my attitude toward teams in the 1970s. It may or may not be a reflection of my feelings in subsequent decades or today.

For example, right now, it is safe to say that I would rather chew on broken glass than see the New England Patriots win another Super Bowl. Living in Connecticut for many years and having to endure the Patriots piling up playoff win after playoff win against the Steelers, there is, I believe, a legitimate basis for this feeling. Forced to exist among the condescending, front running, Millennials and Gen Zers that hopped on the Brady-Belichick-Gronk axis of evil bandwagon, while all along having no clue that their beloved Pats, led by the chicken-necked Steve Grogan, had been slapped around for sixty minutes by the Chicago Bears in Super Bowl XX has been, as they say, no picnic. And even though both Brady and Gronk have left the northeast and been delegated to the National Football League's assisted living program, until the specter of the Hooded One's mystique completely leaves Foxborough, it is unlikely that my feelings for the Pats will change anytime soon.

In addition, the San Francisco 49ers arrived at the f'n hated position in the 1980s for similar reasons as the 2000 to present Patriots. Instead of the Belichick-Brady-Gronk triumvirate, the detestable trio out by the bay was composed of Walsh-Montana-Rice.

Given my harshly cynical personality and general loathing of all things labeled "celebrity," the coronation of 49er head coach Bill Walsh as "the Genius" was, by itself, enough to nauseate me. Montana, who was raised right outside of Pittsburgh and went to college at national heartthrob Notre Dame, was the last pick in the third round of the 1979 draft. The Steelers, who would cap off the decade in 1979 by winning their fourth Super Bowl passed on Montana twice, choosing (Who?) Greg Hawthorne in round one of the draft and (Double who?) Zack Valentine in the second round. Hawthorne and Valentine got Super Bowl rings for their mere presence on Pittsburgh's 1979 roster but played only a combined total of eight virtually anonymous years for the Steelers. Nice work, front office!

In a nutshell, however, I hated the 49ers for the same reason as the Forgettable Decade Cowboys (i.e., they seemingly won all the time). The 1980s to mid-1990s was the era where the National Football Conference (NFC) dominated the American Football Conference (AFC) by winning fifteen out of seventeen Super Bowls from their rival conference. The only team able to overcome this NFC hegemony was the hated Raiders in 1980 and 1983. After that second Raiders victory, the NFC rattled off thirteen straight wins in the big game. This was the era when the Denver Broncos and Buffalo Bills consistently represented the AFC and offered themselves up as cannon fodder for the NFC's big guns. The 49ers, in that seventeen-year time span, won five Super Bowls.

If I am being totally honest, now that I think of it, the statistic that is the lynchpin for my utter disdain for the gold and red pig skinners whose home sits happily on the center of the San Andreas fault, was the five Super Bowls. More than the obnoxious and pretentious "Genius" label, more than Montana's abandonment of western Pennsylvania, surpassing the Steelers in Super Bowl wins was the capstone to my hatred of the 49ers.

Still further, the sting from the fifth 49er Super Bowl win was exacerbated the following year as Pittsburgh attempted to even the score in Super Bowl XXX and fell short when soon-to-be journeyman quarterback Neil "Don't let the door hit you in the ass" O'Donnell *twice* mistook Dallas cornerback Larry Brown for wide-open Steelers receivers and *twice* threw sideline warm-up passes to the singular standing Brown. The second interception came with just over four minutes left in the game, with the Steelers having reduced a thirteen-point deficit to three points, and beginning what could have been at least a game-tying and possibly game-winning drive.

Fifth, while my love of the Yankees, Pirates, and Steelers has legitimate familial roots, there was another trend among my friends, and, I assume, many fans in the Forgettable Decade, that prompted them to latch on to teams outside of the New York metropolitan area.

The football Giants, since 1964, had been mired somewhere between the middle of the pack and Dante's Ninth Circle of Hell. This trend would continue throughout the 1970s and into the early 1980s. The Jets, after their storybook win over the Baltimore Colts in the 1969 Super Bowl (for the 1968 season) had one more season of playoff football in them the following year, losing to the Kansas City Chiefs, the eventual Super Bowl champion, in the divisional round. From 1970 on, however, like their crosstown rivals, the Jets slid into oblivion.

The timing of the two teams' descent into the bowels of competitive professional football is important. In the 1970s the Giants kept their fans' heads spinning by jumping around and calling a variety of different football venues home. From Yankee Stadium to the Yale Bowl in New Haven, Connecticut, to sharing that notorious wind tunnel, Shea Stadium, with the Jets, the Giants carpetbagged around the greater New York metropolitan area, until finally moving to the spanking new Giants Stadium at the Meadowlands across the Hudson River in East Rutherford, New Jersey, in 1976.

At the time, in fact from 1973 forward, the National Football League and television network blackout rules that were in effect required that a team's Sunday home game tickets be sold out seventy-two hours in advance of kickoff in order for the game to be shown on the national affiliate television stations (the pre-1973 rules were actually stricter). Also, back then, there was a clear distinction in the coverage of conference football. CBS aired NFC games while NBC held the contract as the AFC channel.

With both New York teams sucking, the door was open for fans' allegiances to shift to franchises whose games were broadcast on Sundays and actually played football. As a result of these NFL blackout rules, bright lights shined down on teams like the Minnesota Vikings, the Miami Dolphins, the Washington Redskins, the Oakland Raiders, and, in my case, the Steelers. In addition, I believe the blackout policy was a major contributor to the greatest bullshit myth ever pawned off on the US citizenry (i.e., proclaiming the Dallas Cowboys as being "America's Team").

Dallas had been a perennial powerhouse since the 1960s, second only to Vince Lombardi's Green Bay Packers dynasty who had thwarted the Cowboys out of the NFL championship twice in 1966 and 1967. Even with these disappointments, by 1972, Dallas had already appeared in two Super Bowls (V and VI), with split decisions against the Baltimore Colts and the Miami Dolphins, respectively.

While likely an anecdotal memory, on more Sundays than I can recall, Tom Brookshier and Pat Summerall worked the CBS booth, calling Cowboy games and sucking up to the likes of head coach Tom Landry (another friggin' genius) and former Heisman Trophy winner and Naval Academy graduate Roger Staubach.

As a contrast, Major League Baseball had no such problems with games being blocked to audiences. WPIX, Channel 11, carried Yankees games, and WOR, Channel 9, was the Mets affiliate. NBC and ABC got into the act during the decade carrying additional games with special broadcasts like the *Saturday Game of the Week* and *Monday Night Baseball.*

The stage was therefore set for baseball fans to become acolytes of one of the hometown teams, while football fans gravitated to national franchises in cities that were competitive. Jets and Giants fans that remained loyal during the Forgettable Decade were composed mostly of the delusional and self-flagellating.

As a result of the synchronicity of Jets-Giants *patheticness*, many of my friends adopted teams from other cities. I do not consider this front running as it is a natural phenomenon that spans other disciplines. In science, for example, hydrology tells us that water seeks its own level. For 1970s New York football fans, adopting other teams was the life preserver that kept them from drowning.

Sixth, it is equally important to note that, when I say I hated or fucking hated these teams, it is no reflection on the players from opposing rivals as individuals. Plus, among my three best friends were a Raider, a Viking, and a Cowboy fan, and I spent the majority of the Forgettable Decade in their presence.

Yes, I hated these teams' offensive lines, running backs, and wide receivers, and I despised their quarterbacks. On defense, I abhorred their linemen, linebackers, cornerbacks, and safeties. On special teams, their punters were dicks and their kickers were assholes. As mentioned above, it is a fan's right, nay, obligation to hate their team's opponents. The closer in competition between teams, the deeper the hatred.

However, this is not to say that off the field, I might have enjoyed a beer with Jack Tatum, George Atkinson, Phil Villapiano, Tony Dorsett, or Roger Staubach. Well, maybe not Atkinson. But watching them play, on any given Sunday, I wanted their shoulders to separate from their sockets and their knees to go pop.

There is one additional and important element that I should mention to conclude this dissertation on '70s fan dictum that does not lie with the general core of fan lore and was one that, as far as I can tell, was unique to me. This facet of my sports personality formed in the Forgettable Decade and carries through to the present day. It is my aversion to the color royal blue and, with it, the franchises that attire themselves in that color.

In today's university campus parlance, teams that donned this regrettable hue on the playing field—for example, the New York Mets— were tantamount to a microaggression. Likely, this trigger manifested itself as a result of the Mets' 1969 World Series win and the ensuing ridicule I had to endure from contemptible classmates. The situation would continue until game seven of the 1973 fall classic when the Oakland A's vanquished the detestable baseballers from Queens, and the Mets would disappear from the radar for over a decade.

Not limited to the Mets, however, the ailment quickly spread to other leagues and franchises. The Los Angeles Dodgers and Kansas City Royals come to mind. The affliction has also damaged any possible connection I could have with teams like the Buffalo Bills, the pious Montreal Canadians, and, to an extent, even the hometown (albeit Long Island) New York Nets. Especially, after they traded away Dr. J.

It appears also that this infirmity likely has some epidemiological aspect to it, as any relationship I might have with the Los Angeles Rams has been hindered over the years by the constant back-and-forth the team has employed between royal and navy blue jerseys. And, more telling as to the long-term infectious nature of the condition, just because the Denver Broncos switched permanently from royal to navy in 1997, it doesn't get them off the hook. I still don't give a shit about the Broncos.

However, as with any malady, there may also be a bit of natural resistance in effect. For some reason, the New York Rangers have been immune from contamination. Perhaps, the horrible alternative, becoming an Islanders fan, has prevented any of the symptoms from presenting themselves. Like a sports fan's equivalent of the dormant chickenpox virus, it remains in its preshingles state with regard to the Broadway Blueshirts.

As I said, being a fan is complicated stuff.

Chapter 3
New York Pedigree

Bronx Roots

Having recently gone through another exercise that is our nation's de-cennial census, and, given that the outcome of said census is critical for determining eligibility and funding for a variety of federal programs as well as enumerating the population statistics that are the basis for Con-gressional representation, I am, to say the least, skeptical of the process.

Having done a portion of the research for this book by exploring both my Italian and Slovak ancestors, census information from the 1920s to 1950 clearly reveals that census workers, at least back in the day, were either stupid, lazy, or extraordinarily careless. Perhaps all three. They were certainly insensitive to new immigrants that came to the US in hopes of the American dream, most of whom had names that did not match up cleanly with the Smiths, Parkers, or Sullivans from generations past.

My paternal family name, when my Italian grandfather stepped ashore in New York City from a ship named *Cedric*, which embarked from Naples on March 7, 1908, was reported accurately on the ship's manifest as "Antonio Balena." There was no Andolini/Corleone mishap at Ellis Island like in the Francis Ford Coppola classic. However, for the 1920 census, a new incarnation of the name, "Belano," was recorded with family members listed as "Antonio, Fortunati, and James." My grandmother's name was Fortunata. The ship that she arrived on, the *San Guglielmo*, which also sailed from Naples but embarked six years later in 1914, has her name incorrectly on the manifest as Maria Perrotta, using her middle name as her given name. My grandparents were married on November 9, 1916, in the Bronx, with the borough's marriage register listing him as, what looks like from the handwriting, Antonio Balene and my grandmother as Fortinati Perotti.

My father, born Vincenso Balena, on November 2, 1919, used to tell me how, at the time, people named Vincenso, rather than being nicknamed "Vinny," were referred to as "Jimmy." Perhaps, in fairness to the census taker, his screw up (I assume he was back then) came as a result of trying to understand my grandparents' broken, if not totally absent, English.

However, not to let these bureaucrats off the hook completely, in 1930 the trio appeared as "Anthony, Jimmy," and, although my grandmother probably never mentioned the works of Edgar Allen Poe to the crackerjack *federale*, "Fortunato." Ten years removed from the last census, our surname now appeared as "Bellaino."

Just in case you think things get better with time, the 1940 census appears to get the last name correct, "Balena," as well as my grandfather's name; however, living with him at the time were "Jimmie" and my grandmother, who had evolved into "Bonata."

The 1950 census, the year of my grandfather's death, brought about the current incarnation of the family surname as the census lists "Anthony, Maria F., and James Bellano" as residents. Well, at least they got the number of people right.

The Balena family, now Bellano, which I did not mind, as Balena translates into English as "whale" while Bellano translates as "nice or good year," a preferable nom de guerre in my eyes. The change probably saved me a good bit of grammar school ridicule as well. The family made their homes at various addresses in the Bronx, including Third Avenue and Morris Park, but primarily at 1420 Prospect Avenue. I can remember at the time *The Godfather* came out and I had a strong curiosity in all things Cosa Nostra, my father would tell me that one of the neighborhoods of his youth was "Dutch Schultz's territory."

My father served in World War II as a waist gunner on a B-24, *Liberator*, one of the American workhorse, long-range bombers, and flew over twenty missions dropping payloads on German and German-held railroads and munitions factories throughout the Third Reich, while taking on enemy fire from der Fuhrer's 88-mm antiaircraft guns. In a diary he kept to chronicle his missions, he referred to these projectiles from exploded ordnance as "flak."

He was awarded the Air Medal for his service and after V-E Day was shipped to Seattle by train in anticipation of an invasion of Japan. Fortunately, Tojo and the Empire of the Sun tossed in the towel prior to my father's embarkation to the Pacific Theatre.

My father was a guy that could fix anything and was adept at any type of work, all of which he would undertake and complete with perfection. This included electrical, all types of mechanical, automobile, plumbing, and masonry. After the war, and flirting with going into the bar/restaurant business as some of his uncles and cousins had, he chose to utilize his natural aptitude in the mechanical arts to go and work as, what was called at the time, a "refrigeration man" for the Great Atlantic & Pacific Tea Company. More familiarly known as the A&P, this supermarket behemoth at one time had more stores than the top ten US grocery stores in operation today, combined. This range encompasses everything from cavernous Walmarts to the pretentious and overpriced Whole Foods and everything in between.

Shortly after my grandfather's death and while working in Manhattan at one of the stores in his territory, he met my mother, Margaret Lukas, by now, a twenty-six-year-old meat department worker who, about ten years earlier, had left western Pennsylvania to join her older sister in New York in order to survive the lingering impacts of the Great Depression and send some financial assistance back home to her family. They met. They dated. And on May 5, 1952, they were married back in my mother's hometown of Republic, Pennsylvania.

The Terrace City

Yonkers is a suburb of New York City located just north of the Bronx line. It is, or was, in the '70s, a mix of urban and suburban neighborhoods, with the western side of the city being older and having been heavily developed over a time that spanned from the Industrial Revolution through the post–World War II emergence of the American Century. As all places in the northeast US tend to have some connection to colonial America, the city's name is derived from the Dutch, "Jonker," meaning squire, or esquire, or young gentleman, or Dutch middle class, or something like that. The Dutch, like the Swedes and the French, had established colonies in North America in the seventeenth century until the British, as was their modus operandi in those days, came along and absorbed them into the empire. However, as with Quebec and the area known as New Sweden, the Dutch were allowed, for the most part, to remain in possession of their holdings and operate under similar life circumstances as they did before the House of Hanover grabbed it from them.

As an illustration, surnames like Van Cortland, Philipse, Bronck (as in Bronx), and Stuyvesant pepper the area and remain in use in one form or another to this day. Nautical references such as Spuyten Duyvil, the "Zee" in Tappan Zee, and any place ending in "kill" (e.g., Fresh, Wall, Peeks, and Fish) endure today just as they did around the time Peter Minuit unknowingly pulled off the greatest coup in the history of New York real estate from the Lenape Indians.

Despite being geographically in Westchester County, because of its proximity to New York City and easy, direct access to Grand Central

Station via Metro-North's Harlem and Hudson lines, Yonkers is sometimes called, colloquially, the Sixth Borough. This moniker was also probably perpetuated by other Westchester residents from places like Scarsdale, Hartsdale, and Chappaqua, who wanted no association with the place. Yonkers is also known as the Terrace City. Anyone traveling south on the Saw Mill Parkway between Lockwood Avenue and Palmer Road can simply look west to see the scalloped landscape dotted with houses. I am told it is also referred to as the City of the Seven Hills, but nobody that I knew or hung out with ever called it that. The American version of Rome, it was not.

Bounded by the Hudson River on the west and the Bronx River on the east, and bisected by the New York State Thruway, if Yonkers were a grid, it would be roughly divided into the following four areas: northwest, southwest, southeast, and northeast.

As mentioned above, both "wests" were older and more urban, more Bronx or Brooklyn-like, if you will. It was an area of town to which my friends and I rarely ventured as it was considered at the time "the bad part of town." For reference, think New York City circa Jimmy "Popeye" Doyle and *The French Connection*, but without the subway chase.

The one exception was during high school lunchtime when we would occasionally head down to Willow Street to Landi's Deli to feast on one of his famous wedges, our name for a hero or submarine sandwich. This mammoth offering was about eighteen inches long and would be compiled in assembly-line fashion. First, the owner, Frank, would cut the bread and slice the cold cuts. There was a rumor that on occasion Frank would perform the lengthwise cut on the bread using his rather long fingernails instead of a knife, but there are no actual witnesses to this practice.

The next step on the assembly line would be Frank's wife, who would shout, at a level ten decibels higher than necessary, "Ya want some spices?" At this stage, mustard, mayonnaise, oil, vinegar, and a choice of salt, pepper, oregano, and whatever else was lying around could be added. The final step was to pass the wedge on to a guy that we assumed was Frank's brother-in-law but was never fully identified, and who promptly put the enormous submarine sandwich in a bag. I can't remember who took the money for the food, maybe Frank's wife. The purported brother-in-law never struck us as being the sharpest knife in the drawer, so I doubt it was him. However, a Landi's wedge in the late '70s cost about two dollars, so who knows.

Upon entering the deli, we would always ask Frank two threshold questions before ordering: (1) "Frank, do you have roast beef today?" and (2) "Frank, where's the cat?" As to the first inquiry, soft-spoken Frank's response was always, "Sorry, fellas. Only on Monday." While we never, as far as I can recall, ever ventured down to Landi's on a Monday, we asked anyway, just to hear the answer and be amused as only teenagers can. The location of the cat, however, was more of a health-related question as it was widely believed that the feline enjoyed lying on the ham from time to time. Frank's response to the second query was always, "Oh, she's around." Our typical retort? "I'll have the turkey."

Southeast Yonkers bordered the Bronx and Mount Vernon and was where a lot of my uncles and aunts called home and where most of my cousins grew up. It had been developed in the first wave of post-WWII migration that led to the suburban boom of the '40s, '50s, and '60s. It was also the area that, prompted by decades of redlining, led to the controversial, hard-fought, and landmark Yonkers desegregation case of the 1980s.

I grew up in northeast Yonkers, north of Yonkers Raceway and above the Cross County Parkway, the rough dividing line between the eastern sections of the city. This part of town represented the second wave of suburban sprawl from the city with most of the houses being built in the late '50s and early '60s, where the southeast homes were constructed about a decade or more earlier.

The population was made up of mostly second-generation European Americans who had been born in the US and whose parents had emigrated from, mostly, Italy and Ireland, and were overwhelmingly Roman Catholic. There were some Polish and German Americans sprinkled throughout, and a substantial number of Jewish families, who very well could have been either of Polish or German descent. African Americans were virtually nonexistent in our neighborhoods and would not be seen until high school, further results of insidious practice of redlining that had been flagrant for many years and that had been carried to northeast Yonkers by the real estate brokers and lending institutions of the day. Most of the Black kids in Yonkers lived on the west side of town or in the more western sections of the northeast quadrant of the Yonkers grid. A handful of Asian American families appeared in high school as well. The only interactions we had with Latinos, who had not yet made the move from the city to suburbs, would be in the stands at major league baseball games or a television airing of *West Side Story*.

The history of my New York heritage flows through my Italian American father's aforementioned family's journey. It is important to note that, in addition to living through extremely difficult times, an odyssey that was exceptionally challenging, it was not tragic and desperate in a way that was experienced by my mother and that which I will describe in the next chapter.

Reflected in this brief retelling of my family history, whether it be the New York or Pennsylvania branch of the familial tree, I believe it is important to note one of the most admirable characteristics of the Greatest Generation. Those Americans that traversed the difficulties of the Great Depression and World War II did not make it a habit of discussing "family matters," especially ones that were personal, traumatic, and/or embarrassing to the family. Therefore, unlike their Baby Boomer progeny, who wore, and continue to wear, their hearts, souls, livers, kidneys, and large intestines on their sleeves, while engaging in decades-long audible therapy sessions, the Greatest Generation, to put it mildly, kept things close to the vest. Certain things simply went unsaid. Also, there were no camcorders or iPhones back then to document things. A side effect to this approach to life was that some family history ends up being a little spotty.

Despite this somewhat lengthy dissertation on my family's exodus to Yonkers, the fact is, I was the first and only member of my family born there. Both of my sisters had been born and spent at least a few years of their early existence in the Bronx. After their 1952 marriage, my parents rented an apartment in the Morris Park section of the Bronx. Assisted living not being an option at the time, and familial responsibility being paramount among the Greatest Generation, Grandma Bellano lived with them.

My father enrolled and attempted to study engineering at the prestigious Cooper Union for the Advancement of Science and Art on Manhattan's lower east side. Some of you may know Cooper Union as the place where Abraham Lincoln delivered a famous speech in February of 1860. More likely, it will be familiar to others since it is only about three hundred feet walking distance from McSorley's Ale House, the oldest Irish bar in America.

However, the time constraints of working for the A&P and covering a large territory combined with the responsibilities of parenthood (my oldest sister was born in November 1954), while living up in the Bronx, took precedence, and his dalliance with a mechanical engineering degree, a profession he no doubt would have excelled at, ended after one year. As is the case with many of those that lived through that era, when pursuing one's ambitions, more often than not, life and responsibility got in the way. Another stark contrast between the Greatest Generation and Baby Boomers, obligations to family were of more paramount importance than absorption with the self.

In their minds, part of this responsibility involved fleeing the city for the suburbs, getting out of a small apartment for a house and a slice of the American dream, and giving the children the opportunity for a better life than they had.

And so the family moved to Yonkers in what was called the Sprain Lake Knolls neighborhood of the city. The two-bedroom (three, after my father fitted out the attic) split-level abode at 156 Candlewood Drive was purchased in 1960 for $6,000 down and a $16,000 mortgage. I was born there less than two years later. Almost immediately upon moving in, my father, with the help of his cousins and friends, undertook construction and added on a detached twenty-four-by-twenty-five-foot two-car garage.

The split-level homes that dotted the neighborhood came in three styles. Ours had two bedrooms, a full basement, and, initially, no garage. A second model had three bedrooms, an attached one-car garage under the second-floor bedrooms, and a crawl space instead of a basement. The cream of the Sprain Lake Knolls crop had three bedrooms with the same attached one-car garage and a full basement. I had friends that lived in each of the models.

I attended public kindergarten at PS 32, located right up the hill from my house, about one half mile away. Both my sisters and I attended Saint Eugene's Elementary School, a little longer distance, but still only about two miles away. At Saint Eugene's we were taught by both nuns and lay teachers that were, with a few exceptions, always women. The school covered grades one through eight. Navigating through our elementary school years, we would alternate between nun and lay teachers on an annual basis. In fifth grade, some compartmentalization was introduced where both teachers, and, for grades seven and eight, four teachers, would cover the different disciplines of science, English (called language arts), math, and social studies. A homeroom teacher, the class you were actually assigned to, covered one of these core subjects, plus the balance of the day for religion and reading. We had separate teachers for music, art, and gym class. As I will explain later, grade six was an outlier.

There was never an option for me or my sisters to attend anything other than Catholic school. The plan was that we would spend our entire elementary and secondary education there. The assumption was that Catholic schools offered a better and more proven educational atmosphere, allowed for stricter discipline of students and, therefore, either keep everyone in line or threw out the derelicts. Likely, it was a combination of all of these factors. While both of my sisters would stay on this papal pedagogical track, somehow I was able to maneuver toward a different path.

Although I spent one year traveling to White Plains to Archbishop Stepinac High School for ninth grade, the remainder of my secondary education would be spent only a stone's throw from Saint Eugene's at Roosevelt High School, the Theodore Roosevelt High School to be precise.

Roosevelt was located at the busy intersection of Tuckahoe Road and Central Avenue (officially, Central Park Avenue), a major commercial artery that ran from White Plains to the Bronx border. Central Avenue was the epitome of suburban shopping, with strip mall after strip mall lining the length and breadth of both sides of its six lanes and jug-handle U-turns.

Roosevelt's nickname was the Indians. I always thought it was a respectful homage to the history of the area. In fact the "Tuckahoe" in Tuckahoe Road, according to the Encyclopedia Britannica, was named after an edible mushroom like fungi consumed by North American Indians and was also known as "Indian bread." Many of the streets in the area either had Pilgrim-ish (Plymouth, Standish, Bradford, Priscilla, and Alden) or Native American–sounding names (Algonquin, Iroquois, Massitoa, Seneca, and Mohawk).

However, in 2014, the school's nickname was changed to the Sharks, an obvious effort by the Yonkers public school system hierarchy to show sensitivity to Native Americans. And so, rather than continue to demean American Indians, the powers that be chose the name of a Puerto Rican street gang from a Broadway musical to be the mascot of a high school that, according to the website USASchoolInfo.com, has a Latino population of 56.9 percent. Nice work, sensitivity police.

But I digress.

And so, it is within this thumbnail sketch of an existence that my life progressed during the Forgettable Decade. It was, by any measure, a happy existence. This is true even though I had to navigate the trials and tribulations of adolescence, which, as it does for many if not most teens, seems like an arduous trek. And, despite the precarious economic times that accompanied it, while I certainly didn't get everything I wanted, I definitely did not want for anything.

A word of advice to the young people of today as they embark on their nascent life's journey and, who either believe or are told by college professors how difficult their lives are maneuvering through this politically polarized, fast-moving, technology-driven world, take a lesson from the hit single of Bachman Turner Overdrive's 1974 classic album, *Not Fragile:* "You ain't seen nothin' yet."

Chapter 4
The Pittsburgh Connection

Republic, Pennsylvania, is located in the southwestern part of the Keystone State, forty-five miles south of Pittsburgh, thirty-six miles north of Morgantown, West Virginia, and about a million miles from anything resembling civilization. Or, during the times I visited, that was how I saw it.

In the vernacular of Pennsylvania municipal hierarchy, Republic is neither a borough nor a township. While it is generally referred to as a "town," more accurately, and according to the US Census Bureau, Republic is a census-designated place, a moniker as insipid as it sounds. Republic is situated in Fayette County, in the western part of Redstone Township.

At the entrance to the once thriving, now desolate Main Street stands a sign: "Welcome to Republic, The Hub City." "The hub of what?" is now an open question. At one time, I suppose, it was a hub of coal and coke production for the steel industry. For me, when I was visiting the place in the 1970s, I assumed it meant the center of despair. In the parlance of today's government bureaucrats, nonprofit grant writers, and various other societal do-gooders across the political landscape, by all accounts Republic can be designated as a "distressed municipality," but that does not come close to describing what I experienced every summer when visiting my relatives. Republic was, and still is, a poor town. For me, it was Hooterville minus the glamour. Mayberry without all the charm.

A former coal-mining "company town," my mother, her parents, and her siblings grew up in Republic. The history of the American coal industry is readily available in numerous books and documentaries on the subject; therefore, we need not go into a recitation here. Suffice it to say that the boom times that provided immense wealth for the mine owners and operators did not trickle down to the workers. Nowhere was this fact more evident than at 10 Johnson Street in Republic, my mother's ancestral home.

The place was, in a word, sad. My family's personal history was, in another word, tragic. Madness abounded within the house's four walls, and it was where, from the age of eleven months until right before my seventeenth birthday, I spent every one of my summer family vacations. The house, a former coal company home, actually a half house, appeared frozen in time. The interior wallpaper and sheet linoleum, along with the exterior faux brick asphalt siding were probably installed half a century earlier by the minions of coke industry magnate Henry Clay Frick, whose company would ultimately be combined with others to form US Steel.

Southwestern Pennsylvania also had its own, unique dialect. They called soda "pop," (pronounced "pawp") and hero sandwiches (what we in Westchester called wedges) "hoagies." They called lunch "dinner" and dinner "supper." These may seem like minor criticisms, but being from New York, it only added to the oddity of the place.

Without appearing as if I am backtracking, let me be clear: there were cousins, friends, and neighbors that lived in Republic or close by that were not mired in the same depths of poverty that my mother's family was. Their houses were more modern, inside and out. They drove and owned cars. They all held jobs that put them somewhere between the middle and lower-middle working class. All good people.

But the coal industry was so ingrained into the local community that I can recall many occasions where my uncle Joe, when going to the post office (there was no door-to-door mail service) or running to the store, which, by the way is about all that Uncle Joe ever did, would use the phrase, "I'm going 'cross the patch." "Patch" was a euphemism for a long-deceased coal town.

In 1930, at the beginning of the Great Depression, Redstone Township had a population of just over seventeen thousand. By 1970, that number had shrunk to around eight thousand, a decline of 53 percent. In other words, over that time, one way or another, half the population of the area got the hell out. The same, however, could not be said for all of my mother's family.

The Lukas family, in a true Dickensian sense, grew up among heartbreakingly dreadful circumstances. A sort of Slovak *Angela's Ashes* without the booze. This situation greatly impacted the ability of the family to thrive either financially or emotionally as many others could. An extremely religious Roman Catholic family, the living room walls were adorned with portraits of Jesus, Pope Paul VI, and John F. Kennedy, the triumvirate of working-class Catholics. Ironically, however, notwithstanding all of the religious iconography in the house, the situation under which my mother grew up and which I saw on my annual visits could only be described as godforsaken.

My grandparents, John, actually Ján (pronounced Yan) Lukas, actually Lukac, and Anna Matay, actually, Mataj (more US census taker mischief), came to the US at the turn of the twentieth century with millions of other immigrants in a time before the window closed on the tired and poor huddled masses of eastern and southern Europe in the 1920s. As pre–World War I immigrants, John and Anna came to America as Slovak émigrés from the former Austro-Hungarian Empire. Since the Great Powers, in various iterations following the end of the Napoleonic Wars, decided what the balance of power in Europe should look like, John and

Anna had no country, only an ethnicity, to call their own. They were married on November 7, 1916, in Leckrone, Pennsylvania, interestingly ten days before my Italian grandparents did so in New York. John worked in the coal mines, and Anna stayed home and took care of the household and the children.

As for the children, going from oldest to youngest, there was Mary (called Marie), John (named after his father and so really Ján), Margaret (my mother, who always went by Marge or Margie), Agnes, and Joseph. While many Americans of that era had their share of stories of tragedy, distress, and financial woe that accompanied the Great Depression, I believe the Lukases' homelife experiences, compared to others, was particularly harrowing.

There was a sixth child, Anna, born on October 15, 1923, who passed away just seven days later. Almost a year to the day of Anna's birth, October 13, 1924, my mother was born. As mentioned in the previous chapter regarding the Greatest Generation's propensity for discretion, the week that was Anna Lukas's abbreviated life on this earth was barely mentioned among the family. The few times the baby (never referred to as Anna) did come up in conversation, with full Catholic guilt attached, it was lamented that Anna had never been baptized.

The year 1931 was a particularly grievous year for the Lukas family. On February 23, my grandfather, who had, the story goes, lost his leg at some point as a result of a mine accident, took his life. After losing a limb, he was reduced to working more menial jobs. His death certificate states "janitor" at Republic Steel as his occupation. His obituary, more forgiving, lists him as a night watchman. As with many suicides, no one knows for sure the ultimate breaking point, but, perhaps being limited in his ability to work and provide income for his family, combined with the times, the onset of the Great Depression, proved too much for him. Suffice it to say, death by poisoning from drinking a solution of lye dissolved in water—essentially ingesting Drano—and leaving behind a family of six reveals that my grandfather must have found himself in an acutely desperate situation. One where he saw no other way out.

As if that wasn't traumatic enough, less than fifteen weeks later, Johnny Lukas, aged ten, died from complications associated with diphtheria, an extremely virulent bacterial infection that ravaged the United States in the early twentieth century. Young children were particularly vulnerable, and a vaccine did not become readily available until the 1940s.

Left with this desperate situation, my grandmother, obviously of a much stronger constitution than her husband, didn't have the option of taking an easy way out.

Mary, my Aunt Marie, contracted diphtheria the same time as her brother, but survived. As the oldest child, she was charged with making a living and trying to assist the family back home. The 1940 census shows only my grandmother, mother, Aunt Agnes, and Uncle Joe as living in the Republic home. Things were still difficult on Johnson Street as my grandmother is shown on the census as receiving 50 percent or more of her household income from "sources other than money wages or salary" (i.e., sustenance received as a result of the wider social assistance net enacted under President Franklin D. Roosevelt's New Deal). Aunt Marie appears in New York's 1940 census as "Mary Lucas," working as a housekeeper for a family named Rosenberg. At the same time the Nazis had trapped the British and French armies with their backs to the English Channel at Dunkirk, Aunt Marie had already settled in New York City, started making her way in the world, and was sending money home to help out. My mother would join her in the Big Apple shortly thereafter.

Forced to go out into the world far earlier than would be asked of future generations from Baby Boomers to Gen Z, neither Aunt Marie nor my mother finished high school. Both were required to migrate to New York City in their teens where, apparently, work, hope, and familial survival lay. Both women initially worked as housekeepers and nannies.

By 1950, both Aunt Marie and my mother appear in the New York census, living together as "lodgers" and renting a room from a woman named Anna Yefchek (obviously of good Slovak stock) and working in Queens at the Jacoby Bender watchband company. Aunt Marie is listed as an "assembly worker" and my mother as a "foot press operator." Aunt Marie would continue working at Jacoby Bender for the next twenty-five years until she was laid off during the recession of the 1970s. She supplemented her income for as long as I can remember by babysitting, or, as she would call it, "sediet," meaning "to sit" in Slovak.

Aunt Marie lived in Manhattan for the rest of her life, mostly on the upper east side on 69th Street and 1st Avenue. She never married. As an independent woman if there ever was one, she was adored by my daughters, her grandnieces, until her death in 2010.

My mother, sometime shortly after her conversation with that 1950 New York City census taker, landed a job in the meat department at an A&P supermarket in lower Manhattan. The store was one of the supermarkets in my father's territory for refrigeration maintenance. Perchance, they met, and the rest, as they say, is history.

Although I never appreciated it as a child, my mother was, in fact, a remarkable woman. Coming from her meager background, she made her way to the big city, became self-sufficient, married, and raised a family—the only one of the Lukas children to do so. Without a high school diploma, she self-educated herself. I remember seeing her reading the local paper, *The Herald Statesman*, every night from cover to cover, keeping up on the news of the day and clipping coupons for the supermarket. She handled the family checkbook and, in her late '40s, learned to drive. In the stagnant economy of the 1970s, she reentered the workforce part time, to help with family finances. Although Aunt Marie was the older sister, my mother became the anchor of both her family and ours. To the Lukases, owning a home, giving birth to three children, and raising a family, Marge was seen as the apex of success.

On the other hand, Aunt Aggie and Uncle Joe never escaped Republic and stayed in the Johnson Street company home with my grandmother, Jesus, Pope Paul, and JFK for, aside from nursing home stints in their penultimate years, the balance of their remaining days on this earth.

Agnes worked as a nurse's aide until her retirement at nearby Brownsville Hospital, taking public transportation or getting rides from friends for the length of her tenure there. Despite the terrible conditions at home, the hospital must have been a welcome forty-hour-a-week escape for her, as she was extremely well liked at work. In her obituary, her legacy at Brownsville Hospital is described as a person whose "cheery personality made her a favorite of coworkers and patients." Perhaps her time at Brownsville Hospital was an unrealized version of a life that could have been had she not been bound to the indentured servitude of Republic and, like her sisters, was able to escape to a place like New York City. Aunt Aggie always came home with us on our return trip back from vacation, shoehorning into the car, with the expanded passenger list now totaling seven for the eight-hour return trip. She came to New York every summer for two weeks—one week at our house in Yonkers, the other with Aunt Marie in her apartment in the city.

Uncle Joe, on the other hand, was another matter entirely. I could describe him loosely as a less ambitious Eb from *Green Acres*. Happy go lucky and pleasant, especially to his only nieces and nephew, but, to put it lightly, a little off. He ate Kellogg's Corn Flakes out of a huge serving bowl for breakfast and vehemently insisted on having only Carnation Evaporated Milk with his coffee.

As long as my sisters and I made our annual pilgrimage to coal country, Uncle Joe never worked. In 1950, smack in the middle of the post–World War II American century, Joe is listed as "Helper, Candy Shop" on that year's census.

There was a story that he had worked at one time (occupation not specified), but while being driven to work one day by a coworker he put his feet up on the man's dashboard. When asked to remove his feet, Joe apparently threw a tantrum demanding to get out of the car. He walked home that day and did not return to work. There was also a rumor that he had been drafted into the army for service in the Korean War but was designated 4F, unfit for military service. The specifics of both of these stories were never embellished beyond the basics, but like many ancestral legends, they have their basis in fact, with the underlying particulars being left out either as a result of fading memories and/or an attempt to avoid familial humiliation.

A psychological diagnosis today would likely be kind to Uncle Joe, certainly kinder than my Aunt Marie's feelings toward his impoverished but happy-go-lucky lifestyle. Her contempt for him came out regularly in our summer visits. Feeling bad, perhaps guilty, for her sister, Agnes, who carried the financial burden for the Republic household, violent arguments would erupt on a regular basis during our "vacation" time.

Grandma Lukas always sided with Joe. My mother, perhaps embarrassed for this madness to exhibit itself in the presence of her family, consistently tried to keep the peace. Aunt Aggie, meekly, would either stay quiet or, slightly emboldened by her sister's presence, try to assist my mother.

Today, seeing him as the product of an overprotective mother that had lost both the man of the house and a son in a three-month period and growing up in the general dystopia that accompanied living in the household that had experienced such tragedy during the Great Depression, Uncle Joe would certainly be sympathetically diagnosed as having some type of severe emotional disability, one that unquestionably could make him ineligible for both the army and the workforce. As far as I can discern, he had no apparent learning disability. The caption accompanying his high school graduation picture read, "Joe's our mystery man at school. Quiet and dignified. Never a fool." He had a sharp memory and was always up on current events. He could rattle off Pirates statistics like a savant. Maybe he was Redstone Township's version of Rain Man? Aunt Marie just thought he was a bum.

Grandma Lukas lived to the ripe old age of eighty-seven, passing away in March of 1984 and, as it turned out, only predeceasing her daughter, my mother, by nine months.

For entertainment in Republic, we were limited to things like catching lightning bugs in jars with holes poked in the top at night—a very Mayberry-ish thing to do. In order to kill time, we watched local softball and baseball leagues play. Also, we would sit on the back porch, hanging out with the neighbor that lived on the other side of the attached house. Steve Simlavic, a retired miner and former marine, would regale us with stories of the old mining days, when the town was thriving. Mr. Simlavic's home, while separated by only a thin wall from my grandmother's house, was quaint, impeccably clean, and modern. Well, at least 1970s modern. If there was anything approaching entertainment on vacation nights, it came from Mr. Simlavic's well-spun stories.

I can vividly remember one occasion of him detailing the circumstances that led up to the death of United Mine Workers President Joseph "Jock" Yablonski who, with his family, was brutally murdered in their Clarksville, Pennsylvania, home on New Year's Eve, 1969. One evening, he drove us by Yablonski's house, about thirty minutes from Republic, to increase the drama surrounding the incident. On another occasion, he took us to shoot a .22-caliber pistol at an old coke pile. It was the first and only time in my life that I have fired a gun.

From my adolescent perspective, for my parents, the trip to the Republic was not a vacation at all, but this was a myopic view of what vacation should be from the eyes of a spoiled late Baby Boomer versus vacation from the looking glass of Greatest Generation types.

My mother, despite the verbal chaos, I'm sure enjoyed the opportunity to see her mother and family, especially Aunt Aggie, and to visit with cousins that, since her move to New York, had long been in her rearview mirror.

My father occupied himself with what he loved best: working on projects. I'm sure there were many more over the years, but I can specifically recall him installing a bathroom, pouring a slab for the front porch, putting in a bathtub, and replacing the old, galvanized washtub and ringer with a modern washing machine.

For my sisters and me, the annual trip was not so much of a prison term as kids can usually occupy themselves one way or another. More accurately, it was a race. A race to get to sixteen years of age, become eligible for working papers, and procure a summer job. Teen employment was the equivalent of a note from the principal, excusing one from this weeklong class in Dysfunctionality 101. All in all though, we tried to make the best of a bad situation.

On the drive out, my parents tried to soften the upcoming stint in hell by always stopping at a motel around the halfway point, usually either in Harrisburg or Carlisle, for an overnight stay. A kind of calm before the storm, so to speak. We usually stayed under the orange roof of a Howard Johnson, although I can recall a couple of occasions where we stayed at a Holiday Inn. This brief respite before entering the netherworld of childhood vacation allowed us to do nice family things: eating out, swimming in the pool, and just staying at a hotel, which was always a cool thing for a kid to experience in those days. It speaks volumes that the two most enjoyable things about my Pennsylvania vacations, before attending a handful of Pirates games, were the motel stay on the ride out and a stop at Roadside America on the return trip home.

Roadside America was a quaint family attraction off Interstate 78 and located in Shartlesville, Pennsylvania. The attraction boasted a massive eight-thousand-square-foot diorama of a miniature village, complete with a working railroad, a petting zoo, and a nearby gift shop where patrons could pick up everything from cast iron trivets with pithy sayings like, "Bless this house, oh Lord, we pray, make it safe by night and day," to "hex signs," the ubiquitous artwork that adorns barns and houses throughout Pennsylvania Dutch country. Welcoming visitors at the entrance to the building stood two enormous statues of an Amish couple, a kind of oversized Mennonite version of Graham Wood's *American Gothic* in fiberglass.

Since the diorama didn't change much over the years and there was a cost to enter, most years, we would eschew the miniature village and simply use Roadside America as a halfway-point respite. A place to stop, shop a little, eat, and recharge our batteries before the balance of the ride back to New York.

For me, as the Forgettable Decade rolled on, another type of reprieve would be issued that made the trip semibearable. As the 1970s progressed, I was introduced to a shining city on a hill that lay about an hour north of Republic by car. Within this fortress of solitude, Three Rivers Stadium, home of the Pittsburgh Pirates, lay my salvation from both the humdrum and frenzy of 10 Johnson Street.

Chapter 5
Fortunate Son

The old adage holds that you always remember your first time. This is true of your first love, your first sexual experience, which may or may not be mutually exclusive episodes, and the first time you went to a professional sporting event. In my case, this was a New York Yankees game. I suppose there is another category of people that would place theatre, opera, or concerts as of paramount note, but for me, only a baseball game at hallowed Yankee Stadium could rise to the level of a first time worth memorializing. Over the years, my father had instilled in me sufficient enough reverence for the Bronx Bombers to make my maiden voyage to the House That Ruth Built, wildly anticipated and exceptionally special.

While I can only recall flashes of the events associated with that indelible day, I remember them so vividly that it does not diminish the overall importance of the moment. For example, I know the Yanks played the White Sox. Luis Aparicio was playing shortstop for Chicago. There was a short rain delay early in the game, and my childhood idol, Bobby Murcer, was in center field for the Yanks. I can also make an educated guess that I drank soda and had a hot dog and a bag of peanuts. Most importantly, the Yankees won.

Although this rather meager sprinkling of facts might appear to leave fertile ground for embellishment. However, by combining these certainties with a little research, they allow me to complete the full picture of what transpired that day in the Bronx. By using the keen analytical skills I developed over my lifetime and, perhaps more likely, by taking advantage of the magic of the internet, I am able to put together a fuller picture of the game for this writing.

I have determined that my first Yankee Stadium appearance occurred in 1970. How do I know this? First, the White Sox were owned by a showman named Bill Veeck, a kind of P. T. Barnum of baseball that had a penchant for using gimmicks in order to get sports writers talking and fannies in the seats for a franchise that, at the time, had not won a World Series since 1917. Among the gadgets employed by Veeck was to change the team's uniforms every few years. This culminated in the carnival-like purple and white softball uniforms Veeck put on the field in 1976 and that White Sox players and fans had to endure for the next five years. This included embarrassing the players to have to trot around the field in shorts!

At the inaugural game I attended with my father, the White Sox were wearing their road bluish-gray flannels with royal blue caps and socks, a get-up that Veeck decked out the team in during the 1969 and 1970 seasons. In 1971, the Southsiders changed to wearing red caps and socks with a shade of periwinkle blue road uniform. Positive that I did not attend a game in any part of the sixties, 1970 is clearly my universe.

Second, Luis Aparicio was in the lineup that day. Aparicio, a household name shortstop and ten-time all-star, was traded to the Red Sox after the 1970 season, cementing 1970 as the year in question. The plot thickens.

Third, the White Sox came to the Bronx two times in 1970, a three-game series in early June, the fifth, sixth, and seventh, and again in early August for another three-game series. The August series, August 11,

12, and 13, was a series of midweek contests that my father and I would not likely have attended given my dad would have needed to take off work on any of those days.

In addition, the salient point that disqualifies the August series as a possibility comes from the website wunderground.com, which provides historical weather data and shows no precipitation in New York City over those three days.

The reason the game time rain delay is so ingrained in my memory is that anytime the skies opened and one of my Little League games was threatened with being canceled, I would descend into a sort of agitated depression. I would pray to God, asking him, no, begging him, to make the rain relent. If that didn't happen and the Lord gave greater consideration to other matters, like ground well and reservoir recharging or for agricultural benefit, I would proceed to curse the day the universe was created and wonder why my God had forsaken me. Looking back, this behavior was childishly silly, as the game would surely be made up another day shortly thereafter. Then, I would have to report my transgression to a priest in the confessional box within the month, albeit, by downplaying the theatrics by going in with the standard, "I took the Lord's name in vain."

The wunderground.com site shows precipitation on both June 5 and 6 with June 7 being a dry day in the city, narrowing the choices further. The cloudburst on Friday, the fifth, however, occurred in the morning. According to the site, rain on June 6 came around 2:00 p.m., perfectly in concert with one of the handful of vivid memories I have of that day.

So, as it turns out, my baptism to Yankees and major league baseball took place on Saturday, June 6, 1970. Looking back on the box score, the memory is reinforced as the Yankees won that day, 3-1. The Yanks sprayed eight hits over the eight and a half innings it took to dispatch the White Sox. Murcer went one for four. His single, subsequent stolen base and run scored certainly would have made that seminal day more euphoric.

I may be biased, but, to me, there is nothing that compares to a kid's first time going to a major league baseball game. Especially one where their favorite team is playing. I think this was particularly true in my case, getting the chance to visit the old Yankee Stadium, the original House That Ruth Built, where my father heightened the atmosphere and the anticipation with tales of the Babe, the Iron Horse, and his idol, as well as the idol of most Italian Americans of the era, the Yankee Clipper, Joltin' Joe DiMaggio.

The area surrounding Yankee Stadium, even today, hasn't experienced what one might call a renaissance. And, depending on your views about gentrification, the South Bronx has not undergone a revival to the extent that other New York City neighborhoods like Harlem, Park Slope, or Bedford-Stuyvesant have. This was certainly more so in the 1970s, where one could imagine Paul Newman or Al Pacino on a stakeout near 161st Street and River Avenue in their respective *Fort Apache* and *Serpico* days. There were also the interior sections of the vaunted edifice, the wide walkways and souvenir and food stands that, unlike today, served up only the most basic of ballpark fare. Traversing this path before heading to one's seats was no picnic either.

Yankee Stadium opened in 1923 and the almost half century of wear and tear was noticeable, if not obvious. While there was the natural buzz in the hallways that accompanies all pregame anticipation, I remember the interior being dark and a bit dank. I suppose forty-eight years of spilled beer and condiments seeping into concrete were beginning to take a toll. In the days before the Americans with Disabilities Act, if you had tickets in the mezzanine or upper deck, you had to amble up an ever-slowly inclining ramp. This dark, circular trek that, depending where the seats were, was akin to walking around a Cold War era, East German version of the Guggenheim.

However, once you got to your section and began walking out of the tunnel toward your seats, the experience was breathtaking. The visual dichotomy from the interior of the stadium to one's seats was as stark and exciting an event as when Dorothy Gale opened the door to her tornado-transported farmhouse and saw the magnificence of Oz for the first time.

The finely manicured grass contrasted starkly with the smoothly swept rusty tan of the infield and warning track. The transition between brown to green was particularly abrupt compared to the dust bowls that were the baseball fields we played on. Assuming it was a cost-and-maintenance-savings attempt to combat the stagflation of the Ford-Carter era, most of the fields we played on had all-dirt infields. Finally, there was the Yankee Stadium facade. The famous frieze that ringed the top of the stadium transformed what, after all, was really only a ballpark into the modern incarnation of the Roman Colosseum.

As we got to our seats, my father brought my attention toward the right field sky and emphatically made the point that, while no one had ever hit a ball *out* of Yankee Stadium, on a few occasions, Mickey Mantle had hit the facade. The point was elucidated by the fact that on one occasion, the ball was rising as it hit the facade, and, if it hadn't smashed into the decorative cornice, the ball would have hit a subway train or landed on 161st Street.

And so, the question from chapter 1 is answered in full. My 1970s began on June 6, 1970. To my father, a World War II veteran, that date probably sparked memories of D-Day and the Normandy invasion. For me, however, it will always and only be the day I saw my first Yankees game.

Sometimes, You Remember Your Fourth Time Too

While I attended a few games between my inaugural trip to Yankee Stadium and June of 1972, I have little memory of those contests on that hallowed diamond. Typically, my father would take me to a couple of games a year. This was the case until I was old enough to navigate the New York subway system with my friends, or we were old enough to drive to the ballpark ourselves. One thing I do remember about those games is that the Yanks won. My record for in-person Bronx Bombers games remained unblemished well into the 1980s.

The reason the Wednesday, June 14, 1972, game is the next recallable one in my memory is that it was a rather unique experience. My mother took me to the game.

Unlike my first foray, determining the actual date of the game is much easier to identify. No need for me to comb through weather reports to determine precipitation times and levels. Once again, the opponent was the Chicago White Sox, but this time, it is easy to see that Chicago was in the Bronx for two series that year—a midweek series in mid-June and the other right before Labor Day. By 1972, the White Sox were no longer clad in gray flannel and royal blue, but rebranded in light-blue uniforms with red caps, socks, and lettering.

The Labor Day contest was too close to school for me to have gone; plus, that was a weekend series and so my father would have certainly taken me. The Tuesday through Thursday, June 13–15 series, again, would have been one where my father was working and unable to attend. I can best assume that these weekday tickets were given to my father from someone from work or a friend, as normal seating for my family would have been in the mezzanine or upper decks, more reasonably priced tickets. But these seats were field level, midway down the third-base line, and about twenty rows behind the visiting team's dugout. For a twelve-year-old, it was Nirvana, Valhalla, and Elysium all rolled into one. Catholic heaven of the type the nuns at Saint Eugene's spoke about would have put the seats behind the Yankees dugout.

Two factors dictate the certainty that it was the Wednesday game. First, the Yanks lost the Tuesday contest 2-0, so that one is out. Second, the Yankees won the Thursday game 8-1, with Bobby Murcer leading the way with a three-run blast in the second. Although Murcer hit a solo shot in the game I attended, if I had been there on the fifteenth, I certainly would have remembered, and treasured, such a memory. The game I attended was not a huge blowout.

However, one of the seminal moments that cements Wednesday as the day in question is that before the game, the players were hanging around the White Sox dugout, talking to fans and signing autographs. These were still the days when pro athletes didn't try to additionally feather their nests by charging exorbitant amounts of money for memorabilia and autographs. Back then, autographs were seen as a sort of obligation to the fans. Having been blessed with the opportunity to play a child's game into manhood and for a very good living, it was a small inconvenience to bear.

Always keeping score at the game like any dedicated fan of the time and given our seats' proximity to the White Sox dugout, I presented my program and pencil to a Chicago player who wore the number one on the back of his jersey. Initially unable to decipher the signature, the autograph turned out to be that of Luis Alvarado, listed in the program as a shortstop. I had no idea who he was.

Alvarado, a journeyman that played nine years for five different teams, four of them with the White Sox, compiled an unremarkable .214 career batting average. But that didn't matter. For a ten-year-old fan meeting face to face with a major league ballplayer and getting his first autograph, regardless of the fact that he couldn't swat flies, was still magic. It might have well been Lou Gehrig that signed my program that day. Granted, had I shown it to my friends and waved the signature around like a winning lottery ticket, I surely would have been laughed out of the room and skewered mercilessly.

I also remember that Alverado did not start and only got into the game late as a pinch hitter. But I never forgot the generosity and courtesy shown by a big leaguer to a young fan on that day. In my book, Alvarado will always be a good guy.

Yes, the Yankees won that day. Johnny Callison hit a first-inning home run that got the fans jazzed up early and proved to be the game winner. But that is not the importance of the day.

As mentioned earlier, my mom had only gotten her license recently; however, it is uncertain to me what exact mode of transportation we took to the game. Even with my father, a drive to the stadium might not ordinarily be by car. Sometimes, we would drive down to the Woodlawn stop on the Jerome Avenue line and take the number 4 train to the stadium. The only reason I am questioning whether my mother and I also did this is, as a new driver, she might not have wanted to try and navigate the streets around Jerome Avenue and attempt to find a parking space in that congested area of the Bronx. On the other hand, my mother had been in New York for over a quarter of a century and lived in the Bronx since 1952; therefore, she was no stranger to the subway system. We may, however, have parked the car behind Carlo's Italian Restaurant on Central Avenue and Tuckahoe Road and hopped on the number 20 bus that would have taken us right to Woodlawn as well. In any event, we got there. We had great seats, and it was a beautiful day.

In the end, the main reason the game has lodged itself in my consciousness over time was not Bobby Murcer going two for three with a home run, a double, and a walk; Johnny Callison's four bagger; or Mike Kekich's four-hitter. It wasn't even the Luis Alverado autograph. It was the fact that my mother took me to the game.

Bat Day and the X-15

Sixth grade, September 1972 to June 1973, at Saint Eugene's was a watershed year. For starters, it was the grade where the Catholic Church deemed it a propitious time to separate girls and boys in order to teach students the facts of life. The thought was, I assume, that either sociological studies or some Council of Cardinals at the Vatican had determined that eleven- and twelve-year-olds were racing toward the precipice of hormonal rage to such an extent that a yearlong tutorial about the birds and the bees was necessary.

I can only assume that it was by some sort of warped divine intervention that the powers that be doled out the responsibility for teaching sex ed to two of the least-qualified representatives on the planet. For the girls, a nun was assigned to read them the riot act about premarital intercourse and gospel truth about the advantages of the rhythm method. I am speculating here as the girls and guys never compared notes. For the boys, in the eyes of the school leadership, only a first-rate pervert would do for teaching such a delicate topic. And so we found ourselves in the company of Mr. Tom McMann.

While memories of Mr. McMann's pedagogical methods are scant at best, I vaguely remember a 35-mm slide or an overhead transparency depicting both male and female sex organs. But Tom's real expertise wasn't in teaching human reproduction. His acumen lay in being a contemptible reprobate.

McMann was also the adult in charge of an after-school boys group called the Rangers, a kind of head scoutmaster to a group of Boy Scouts. I don't know if it was Tom that came up with the idea of the Rangers so as not to have to answer to some committee or larger organization and keep his activities to himself, but, looking back, it was an odd choice to create this standalone, after-school group.

The physical exercises we performed as Rangers were diagramed on handout sheets and based on the regimen developed by the Royal Canadian Air Force (RCAF). I haven't a clue whether Mr. McMann had determined that United States Air Force jumping jacks, squat thrusts, and other calisthenics were so intrinsically flawed that he had to adopt the RCAF model, but I am certain that, in a prior life, there was no way

McMann had learned the exercises serving as a flyboy for the Canadian military.

Tom's perversion was exemplified in three ways. First, after exercises and activities, Tom would supervise massages among the Rangers, having us boys buddy up with one another and rub each other down with witch hazel and other masseuse-related accoutrement. The kicker was, for some reason, McMann felt it necessary for us to monitor each other's internal body temperature by use of a rectal thermometer.

Second, perhaps for his own visual enjoyment in the privacy of his own home, McMann would photograph members of the Rangers in the boys' shower, clothed only on our athletic supporters. Under the guise of checking to see if our postures were developing on the straight and narrow, he would hang a plumb bob from the locker room ceiling, align it with the center of our bodies, and take pictures from all four angles, facing front, rear, left, and right.

Third, and Tom's real skill, where he was most accomplished, was smacking kids with paddles and other available classroom resources, a kind of Torquemada with a bowtie. For classroom cut-ups, general disobedience, or not paying attention while we were reading passages from the text aloud, Tom had an intricate hierarchy of infractions, all of which would be addressed to the commensurate degree with the appropriate punishment. The litany reads as follows:

1) Smacks on the hand with a ruler (palm up),
2) Smacks on the hand with a ruler (palm down),
3) Hot Dog (smack on the foot with a ruler, sock on),
4) Hot Dog with Relish (smack on the foot with a ruler, sock off),
5) Underwear Bare Bottom, or UBB (smack on the ass, pants pulled down, underwear on),
6) Red Bare Bottom, or RBB (smack on the ass, pants and underwear pulled down).

The latter two punishments were meted out via use of his private inventory of paddles. Some of these were standard fare (e.g., a small canoe oar). Others had names—for example, the X-15 and the Nature Paddle.

The X-15 was a handmade paddle claimed to have been crafted and given to him by a student. The X-15 was fitted with an easy-to-grab handle and drilled through with numerous holes so that air resistance would be at a minimum. The Nature Paddle, a sort of precursor to the modern pickle ball racket, bore an inscription, a kind of degenerate's creed: "Never slap a child in the face, for nature provides a better place."

The crazy thing about this latter practice—the whacks with a paddle—was thought to be cool with the kids in the class, including me and my friends. Since Tom had been engaging in this practice, grade after grade, year after year, there was a sort of rite of passage to get your butt smacked by the X-15.

Pivoting to a more sanguine story from that school year, another notable event was the arrival at Saint Eugene's of a new kid, Vince Morelli. Vince had just recently moved to Yonkers from the Bronx. He had an attractive way about him, a cool kid from the city. Like my father, Vin's dad also worked for A&P as a produce manager, at what my father described as "a vegetable head." I thought that characterization was hilarious, but my dad said it with a straight face, so it was probably a typical colloquialism within the A&P ranks. Vin's dad and mine knew each other for years as my father had regularly visited Mr. Morelli's store to work on a refrigeration unit or freezer that had gone on the fritz.

Unlike my other two stadium excursions mentioned above, there is no doubt or deep research required to confirm the date of the next memorable game I attended. First, 1973 was the last year of the old Yankee Stadium. In 1974, the Yanks would move over to that hell hole in Queens known as Shea Stadium, splitting time with the Mets while the House That Ruth Built got a facelift. The Bronx Bombers would be banished to Shea for two years, culminating in one of the great tragedies in New York baseball history, the trading of Bobby Murcer.

Second, there were two Bat Days that year, but the second was part of a doubleheader against the White Sox in July. The reason for the second giveaway was that attendance at the first Bat Day was so overwhelming that thousands had to be turned away at the gate with hat in hand, but no baseball bat.

I'm not sure whose idea it was, but somehow between the fathers it was decided that a spur-of-the-moment trip to the stadium for a souvenir giveaway day would be a good idea. In those days, every fan, fifteen and under, received a real Hillerich & Bradsby Louisville Slugger bat, complete with a player's signature branded into the barrel and which could actually be used for Little League games. This was a time before either the Yankees got cheap and began meting out smaller replica-sized bats to the first ten, or fourteen thousand, or whatever number of kiddies were deemed worthy of receiving a piece of wood for having *schlugged* their way out to the park. Or, it may have been that, over the years, team ownership feared that thuggish types would attend the game just to beat each other senseless with baseball bats. Maybe it was a little of both. In any event, for many years, future generations of young fans certainly got the shaft when it came to what was, with Old-Timers' Day and the Mayor's Trophy Game (vs. the Mets), one of the showcase games of the year.

Given the real-time decision to head to the game, there was no way tickets were bought in advance. Also, it is extremely unlikely that either Big Jim or Mr. Vegetable Head would have approached a scalper. Given this, the tickets were almost certainly purchased at the box office, and based on the location of our seats, they may have been the last four seats left. It may very well have been that the game was sold out, but then the attendant at the ticket window looked down and realized he had dropped four tickets, stepped all over them, and then reintroduced them for sale just as my father walked up to the window.

In the old stadium, looking from home plate to the left side of the right field foul pole in fair territory lay five sections, numbered 25, 27, 29, 31, and 33. After section 33 was a precipice that dropped to the ground and a gap between the stands and the bleachers. Our seats were in section 31 of the upper deck. If the seats were only at nosebleed height, it might not have been too bad, but as we ascended up the sticky cement steps that were typical of Yankee Stadium, it became clear that these seats were more in cranial hemorrhage territory than nosebleed. We were fortunate, however, in that someone that was seated too close toward right center field in section 33, under the right circumstances, could have easily plunged to their death. To be more specific, the seats were almost directly below the facade where Mickey Mantle, a decade before, had launched what the Mick described as "the hardest ball I ever hit," which my father had pointed out to me at my inaugural game. But Mantle was no longer in pinstripes. In other words, we were a long, long, long way away from home plate. And, in fair territory.

Ever the idealistic fan, I even rationalized that if the right pitch came along, Ron Bloomberg might get ahold of one and launch it into our section. Nonetheless, we were at the Stadium on Bat Day. On second thought, the seats were awesome!

In addition to the high altitude in which our seats were located, there were only two other memories from that day. One, the Yankees won, my record remained intact; and, two, I encountered a situation for which I had to make my first real-life business decision.

Of course there are times when even youngsters have to make something akin to a business decision. Sure, with limited change in my pocket, on many occasions I had to decide whether to get the Chocolate Éclair or go for the Jet Star Popsicle from the Good Humor man, but that was a fairly insignificant transaction compared to what was to transpire in Section 31 that day.

Once, I had undertaken the decision to trade my Topps Sam Mc-Dowell baseball card for a friend's Denny McClain. "Sudden Sam," as he was known, played the majority of his fourteen-year career in pre–Guardian Cleveland for the Indians and had a short stint with the Yanks. Over his career he compiled a 141-134 win-loss record with a career 3.17 earned run average (ERA) and a .513 winning percentage. With five years less longevity, McLain won 131 games against 94 losses, mostly for the Detroit Tigers. Even with a higher ERA, his .590 winning percentage, I believe, tops McDowell stats. Plus, McLain was the last major league pitcher to win 30 games in a season (31 in 1968), so I think I made the right decision. Unless, of course, my friend Gary had *two* Denny McLain cards in his collection.

Walking into the stadium, I was presented with my bat, a Felipe Alou model Louisville Slugger. Of course, I wanted a Murcer bat, but it was not to be. I was happy with the bat. Alou was the oldest of the famous Dominican baseball trio, the Alou brothers—Felipe, Matty, and Jesus. In my mind, he was a solid player and a first baseman, my position, so there was a natural connection.

After arriving at our seats, we found ourselves sitting next to a Latino father and his son. The kid was about my age. I am not sure how the negotiations started or the transaction closed, but within a few minutes, he was in possession of my Alou bat and I had procured a Ron Bloomberg model.

The Yankees won that day 3-2. The box score and a *New York Times* archived article tell me the game was close with the Angels scoring in the top of the ninth with the go-ahead runs left on base. Doc Medich pitched eight innings but allowed the first two batters to get on base in the ninth. Sparky Lyle came on in relief, allowed one run (charged to Medich), and struck out the twenty-seventh out for the win.

Other than the win, all of the other game-time minutiae escape me from that day. But two facts make the game remain in my memory.

Sitting in what today might be called an original "sky box" and the seminal arms-length transaction between an Italian American kid and a Latin American kid that made their day very special.

It may be said that I was a soft touch, giving in to the puppy dog eyes of an Alou fan in exchange for a bat signed by a better-than-average player who hit for high average and had decent power. But as it turned out and unbeknownst to me at the time, Alou, who had originally come up to the majors in 1958, was nearing the end of his career. In September, he was waived by the Yankees, picked up by the Montreal Expos, and eventually landed with the Milwaukee Brewers. His career was over in 1974. On the other hand, Bloomberg, from a historical perspective, was the first designated hitter to step into the batter's box in MLB history. In the end, I think I got the better part of the deal.

I wonder what ever happened to that bat.

Chapter 6

Sanity at the Confluence of the Three Rivers

After many years of following the same old vacation script, my parents, perhaps with the prompting of our neighbor, Mr. Simlavic, came up with an idea to try and make the vacation more like it was supposed to be (i.e., some measure of fun for the kids). The decision was a game changer for me, one that would make the trek to Republic somewhat bearable. In other words, we got the hell out of town.

Some time, probably around 1970 or 1971, a light bulb went off, and the family packed up the car and headed up to an amusement park called Kennywood Park, a kind of Six Flags, or, for my Yonkers and Westchester County contemporaries, Rye Playland, located about twenty minutes southeast of Pittsburgh along the Monongahela River in Mifflin, Pennsylvania.

That summer turned out to be a watershed year. To date, vacation entertainment mostly consisted of the aforementioned men's softball leagues and catching fireflies in a jar in the backyard. Other than that, there were few times that could be considered memorable occasions. Maybe, that trip to the coke pit to shoot Mr. Simlavic's .22 pistol.

I also have a memory of going to the Brownsville Drive-In and seeing *Flaming Star*, starring Elvis Presley. The movie came out before I was born, in 1960. It might have been that the movie had only made its way out to Dullsville, Pennsylvania, a few years after it was released to the rest of the civilized world, or it was part of some comeback tour. My only *Flaming Star* recollection is a small but an extremely vivid one: the ending. After what I suppose was a climactic battle with the bad guys, a gravely injured Elvis rode back to the ranch and was urged by costar, Steve Forrest to come in and get help. Elvis replied, "I saw the Flaming Star of death," which, I guess meant that he was finished. Elvis rode off into the hills…and scene!

Despite it being such a pivotal moment, I also only have limited remembrance from that trip to Kennywood Park. I couldn't tell which rides we went on. However, I recall that Tiny Tim was the feature act at the outdoor theater. Tiny Tim, the stage name of Herbert Khaury, had come into fame at the only time that a long, scraggly haired, ukulele-playing, falsetto-singing, and flamboyantly dressed entertainer could have, the 1960s.

While I cannot recount Tiny Tim's play set, there is no doubt that he performed his biggest hit and signature tune, "Tiptoe Through the Tulips" that day. Cleary, the images of Tiny Tim that we had been exposed to at that point were a bit weird, even freakish, including his marriage on *The Tonight Show Starring Johnny Carson* in 1969 to "Miss Vickie."

The final recollection from that day was a remark my father made about Tiny Tim while driving back from the park to Republic. My father never really had a bad word to say about anyone, at least in my presence. But as a World War II vet and member of the Greatest Generation, I was curious as to what he thought about this anomalous character that had been spawned from the flower child generation. I wasn't looking for the standards like, "Damn hippy," or "He should get a haircut." These were not my father's style. But I was somewhat taken aback by his subtle observation of Tiny Tim, which was, simply, "He seems like a good Joe." High praise indeed from the generation that was known for subtle understatement.

The significance of the Kennywood Park trip was not that we had seen Tiny Tim in person, or for at least one vacation day we had finally gotten out of dodge. Rather, the adventure set off a spark, a spark that must have caught on to the kindling and, when properly stoked in the minds of my parents, came ablaze. Shortly thereafter, on a subsequent trip to southwest Pennsylvania, a new tradition was born: an annual trip to Three Rivers Stadium to see the Pittsburgh Pirates play.

The Lumber Company

The trek from 10 Johnson Street to 600 Stadium Circle, the former site of Three Rivers Stadium, home to both the Pirates and the Steelers from July 1970, when the Bucs opened the new stadium, until December 2000, when the Black and Gold played the last game there, took about an hour. Aptly named, the stadium stood at the convergence of the Allegheny, Monongahela, and Ohio Rivers.

My first soiree to Three Rivers Stadium was an exciting event, as not only was I escaping the red dog roads and coke hills of Republic, but since the Pirates had slayed the Orioles in the 1971 World Series, there was excitement and optimism surrounding the team. On all prior trips to Pennsylvania, the sports buzz was almost exclusively about the Pirates. Prior to 1972, I barely heard the word "Steelers" mentioned among the Republic curmudgeons.

Yes, the Pirates were all the rage when it came to sports discussions in Republic. This is probably because, in addition to the upset of the Orioles, yarns about the team's miracle victory over the Yankees in the 1960 World Series, when Bill Mazeroski hit a walk-off homer off of Ralph Terry in game seven at Forbes Field, were still in the air.

But the team was also on the ascendency. They had won the NL East in 1970, only to be sent packing by the Cincinnati Reds in a three-game sweep in the National League Championship Series (NLCS). The team had also been the first major league franchise to put an all-Black team on the field at one time. On September 1, 1971, the year they would go on to win the pennant and the World Series, the Pirates lineup card on that historic day was as follows:

1. Rennie Stennett 2B
2. Gene Clines CF
3. Roberto Clemente RF
4. Willie Stargell LF
5. Manny Sanguillén C
6. Dave Cash 3B
7. Al Oliver 1B
8. Jackie Hernández SS
9. Dock Ellis P

My first Three Rivers trip was also a very different experience than my first time at Yankee Stadium. Unlike the history and grandeur that accompanied the celebrated Bronx structure, Three Rivers was spanking new. It was one of a series of modern, cookie-cutter stadiums built in the 1960s and '70s to serve the dual purpose of being home to both a municipality's Major League Baseball and National Football League franchises. Along with places like Busch Memorial in St. Louis, Riverfront in Cincinnati, and Veterans Stadium in Philadelphia, these concrete boxes were all offspring of the Houston Astrodome, sans roof. As such, Three Rivers and its sibling edifices all featured artificial turf. Actually, the Pirates played on Tartan Turf, the 3M competitor to Monsanto's more popular Astroturf. Essentially, Tartan Turf was indoor/outdoor carpet laid out over a cement floor. If walking through the tunnel at Yankee Stadium for my first view of the field was like seeing Oz, then doing the same in Pittsburgh was more like arriving on the backlot at Universal Studios. Comparing Three Rivers to the House That Ruth Built was like seeing I. M. Pei's Pyramid juxtaposed against the Louvre.

Clinging to the adage that you always remember your first time, the same holds true for my first foray to Three Rivers. On that day, I couldn't have asked for a better welcome. First, their opponents were the despised Cincinnati Reds. The Big Red Machine had come into town and had already taken the first two games of a three-game series by comfortable margins. Therefore, the game I attended was of major importance. I fucking hated the pompous, clean-cut Reds for the same reasons I would hate teams like the Dallas Cowboys and, later, the San Francisco 49ers (i.e., things always seemed to go their way, and they always seemed to win).

Second, I was extremely fortunate as my favorite Buc, Roberto Clemente, who had been struggling with injuries all year and would only come up to bat a total of 378 times in 1972, was in the lineup. He had not played in either of the first two games of the series. But when we arrived at the stadium, the Great One was batting third and playing right field.

Third, and finally, the Pirates won! The game was one of those hold-your-breath, edge-of-your-seat-type affairs where the Bucs had been knotted up with the Reds 1-1 since the third inning. Then, in the top of the seventh, the goddamn Reds broke through with the go-ahead run. One can imagine, falling behind late in the game to a team like the Reds can be extremely stressful to a fan, especially one at his first home Pirates game. But the baseball gods were with me that day, and the Bucs came up with two runs in the bottom of the eighth, shut down the Reds in the ninth, and stole the victory. Clemente drove in two runs, and Willie Stargell drove in the third.

It was a good thing that the Pirates won that day as my euphoria was short lived that season. The Reds came back in a more critical situation and did what they always seemed to do to my Pirates in that era: deliver a crushing loss.

The next time the Pirates were ahead of the Reds, 3-2 in the ninth inning, was in game 5 of that year's NLCS. The Pirates, only three outs away and with the pennant within their grasp, blew the 3-2 lead at Riverfront. On the edge of whatever I was sitting on that afternoon, I watched as Johnny Bench tied the game with a leadoff, two-strike, opposite field homer off Dave Giusti. This calamity was followed shortly thereafter by a disastrous, two-out, first-and-third, wild pitch by Bob Moose, allowing the winning run to cross the plate. Oh, the humanity!

This devastating outcome further underscores the fact that sports fans, while they can experience fairy-tale endings, can also end up sitting in the front row at the Globe Theatre for a Shakespearean tragedy.

Speaking of tragedy, 1972 would also be Clemente's last year in Pittsburgh and on this earth. On December 31, 1972, the thirty-eight-year-old Clemente sponsored a humanitarian mission for delivering critical supplies to earthquake victims in Nicaragua. The plane tragically crashed into the Caribbean shortly after takeoff. About three months earlier, on what turned out to be his last at bat of the 1972 season, Clemente ripped his three thousandth hit and secured his place among baseball's immortals. He reached this milestone at home and against the Mets.

While I know I attended Pirates games most summers during the Forgettable Decade until I stopped making the trip to Republic, there was one year that we visited when the Bucs were out of town on a road trip. Because the typical time frame in which we frequented the area was late July to early August, we were always at the mercy of the Pirates' schedule.

In addition to the 1972 inaugural Reds game, I attended a second memorable contest in 1975, an 8-1 flaying of the Phillies in a promotional give-away game that only could have taken place in the Steel City.

The famed Babushka Night, July 30, 1975, was a gimmick cooked up by longtime broadcaster Bob Prince, who years earlier had concocted another famous Pirates talisman, the Green Weenie.

Playing the eastern European card and the Babushka Power theme that was prominent during midseventies Bucs games, female Pirates fans were enticed to Three Rivers to join their male counterparts. Pirates fan attendance, even when they were winning, can best be characterized as mediocre. On Babushka Night, however, more than forty-three thousand fans packed the stadium on an evening that otherwise would have drawn a typical midsummer doldrums crowd of a third or half that number.

The atmosphere was electric. It was an amazing night and a decisive win featuring throngs of women waving their head scarves around. However, to be honest, Bat Day, it was not.

One game I attended, I don't remember which, I recall that Richie Zisk, who had the unenviable task of trying to fill Roberto Clemente's cleats in right field, had a big game. Despite this precarious situation, Zisk was, nevertheless, a popular player with the fans during his tenure with the Bucs. My belief was that because his name had a "Z" and "k" in it, the fans thought he must have been of Eastern European descent, perhaps even Slovak.

In any event, from 1972 through 1977, besides the Reds and Phillies, I know I saw them square off against the Cardinals and Cubs. In 1977, I drew such a short straw that I had to sit and watch the Mets when they came to town. I couldn't tell you which Mets game I attended, but it is easy to document that it was a Pirates victory. Another reason that summer sticks out in my mind is that the infamous Son of Sam, the .44 Caliber Killer, who had terrorized New York City for the past year, was captured and brought into custody. The Bucs won seven of eight games during David Berkowitz capture week, including a five-game sweep of the Mets.

Besides the Reds and Phils, I only remember flashes from the balance of these contests. I know the teams that they played but couldn't tell you what specific day they played them. Also, unlike my unblemished appearances at Yankee Stadium, I distinctly remember one of the games being a loss—I think the Cardinal game—prompting a long, depressing ride from Three Rivers back to Republic.

Never, Ever Leave Early

The only other in-person Pirates game that holds a memorable place in my mind from the Forgettable Decade is one that does not have a happy ending. In fact, this regrettable incident did not even occur at Three Rivers. It happened at that loathsome transfer station masquerading as a ballpark known as Shea Stadium. That night, I was introduced to one of the cardinal rules of fan parenting; an edict that has stayed with me my whole life and where there is almost no room for compromise. Never, ever leave a game early!

Of course, my animus for Shea dates back to the 1974 season when Yankee Stadium was undergoing a two-year renovation and the Bombers were forced to play in Queens. Without the iconic 296-foot short porch that Yankee Stadium's right field featured, an exceptional advantage for lefty hitters like Bobby Murcer to spend 81 games a year, and due to the persistent swirling winds that by the seventh inning brought all types of garbage rolling across the field like tumbleweed refuse, that year in Queens sounded the death knell of my idol's tenure for the Bronx Bombers.

Murcer's 1974 numbers—ten homers, eighty-eight RBIs (runs batted in), and a .274 batting average—were not terrible, but they were not the type of statistics that were expected of such a highly paid Yankees star. With the prospect of a second year at Shea looming, Yankees owner George Steinbrenner, never shy about taking any opportunity to make a headline, sent Murcer packing to the San Francisco Giants for 30-30 superstar Bobby Bonds.

However, because of the financial situation that confronted most 1970s teenagers, I found myself going to a number of Mets games mid-decade, mainly for two reasons.

First, the tickets were cheap. After appearing in the 1973 World Series against the juggernaut Oakland A's, the Mets, as was, and still is, their penchant, fell into limbo. In 1974, just a year removed from the pennant, the "Amazins" finished five games out of the cellar and seventeen games behind the division-winning Pirates. In 1975, they finished third, ten and a half games behind the Buccos, and in 1976, while on their way to again finishing third, ended up a full fifteen games behind the division winner, the Philadelphia Phillies.

Due to this sharp decline in both success and talent, Mets tickets became readily available and were relatively affordable. In order to drive interest, the team even went so far as to cook up a promotional deal with Dairylea, at the time the largest milk distributor in the tri-state area, to put Mets tickets coupons on the company's milk cartons. The theory went, I suppose, the more Dairylea milk you drank, the stronger your bones would get, and the more Mets coupons you could redeem for tickets. Yes, a decade before lost and missing children began appearing on milk cartons, it was preceded by another humanitarian venture (i.e., offering tickets to lost and missing Mets fans).

Second, one of my good friends at the time was a Jewish kid that lived a few houses away. Like me, Gary, was a diehard Yankees fan, but as I observed with other young Jewish boys my age, they had a sophistication with regard to knowing their way around New York City, including the use of Gotham's graffiti-filled and urine-soaked transit system, the New York Subway. Gary knew that once we made our way from the number 20 bus to Woodlawn and the number 4 train to Grand Central, we could then hop on the 7 line to Shea and cash in on our Dairylea tickets.

But my memorable game discussed here was not the product of milk carton tickets. A neighborhood friend's father, you know, one of those friends that you spend quite a bit of time with when you are young likely due to the proximity to one's own home and then drifts away and becomes a memory as time passes and you gravitate elsewhere, got tickets to the September 20, 1976, game at Shea against the Pirates. Whether Mr. Dumont knew I was a Pirates fan and, therefore, invited me along or just had an extra ticket, I could not say.

September 20 of that year was a Monday, and it was a night game. As far as I can tell, Tuesday was a regular school day. Just weeks before, I had escaped the shackles of Catholic school education and began my coeducational tenure at Roosevelt High School. Most likely, however, the tickets became available and I was going with another parent, so my mother and father did not have a problem with my going to a game on a school night.

To further enhance the allure of this Monday night contest, the Pirates, between 1970 and 1975, won the National League East every year with the exception of 1973. As mentioned earlier, that year, the Bucs finished in third place but only two and a half games behind the Mets, the National League's eventual pennant winners. Unbeknownst to me at game time, the Pirates were about to begin a three-year hiatus from the postseason. The Philadelphia Phillies had wrested control of the National League East in May and had maintained and lengthened their lead throughout the summer.

At the time, the Phillies had never won a World Series. Their last appearance was in 1950 when they were swept in four games by the Yankees. Since then, their closest flirtation with the postseason play was in 1964 where, despite being six and a half games in front with twelve left to play, they collapsed and forfeited the pennant to the St. Louis Cardinals. What made the Monday night Mets-Bucs game so intriguing is, at that juncture, it appeared that the Phillies might be reliving 1964, this time to the benefit of their Keystone State rivals.

On August 13, 1976, the Phillies had a thirteen-game lead over the second-place Pirates. By September 1, it had shrunk to nine and a half games. On September 15 it was down to five. When the Buccos took the first game of the four-game series against the Mets, it was down to three. After dropping the next two games to the friggin' Metropolitans, at game time on Monday night, from our seats slightly offset to the first base side behind home plate and in the upper deck, the Pirates sat four games out with the Phillies idle that night.

And why is this game so memorable? No, not because the loss sent the Bucs on a downward spiral and to a depth from which they would not be able to climb back up for three seasons. Sure, losing sucked and losing to the Mets sucked more, but that was not the seminal moment that occurred that night.

As stated above, one of the fundamental principles of the fan canon, a rule that should never be deviated from except under the most serious of circumstances, is the dictum that one must never leave a game early. This is true even in instances of inclement weather (you can find cover if necessary), or a blowout loss (you'll get them next time, so stand by your team). The birth of a child—your child—may be an acceptable excuse. A death in the family might be an allowable explanation, but it clearly depends on the relationship to the individual and the timing of the heavenly departure.

For example, I cannot imagine calling or texting someone at a Yankees-Mets interleague subway series game to tell them Cousin Minnie, twice removed, had passed and expect a prompt departure from the stadium. So as not to sound too harsh or irresponsible here, the reader must remember that, during the Forgettable Decade, an era before the cell phone had entered our lives, there would be no way of contacting a family member and bringing news that either birth or death had occurred.

"Daddy, where were you when I was born?"

"Well, honey, Ron Guidry was working on a two-hitter against the Brewers…"

The philosophical question, therefore, is, should we allow technology, just because it exists, to spoil our fun? One of these situations came up for me when I had to leave the Meadowlands early in the third quarter of a Steelers-Giants game to pick up my daughters from the babysitter. Knowing that a strict time frame was in effect, I was forced to leave the Black and Gold at halftime with a tenuous 20-14 lead. As it turned out, I would miss an up-and-down second half, one in which the lead would change hands four times, culminating with the Bus, Jerome Bettis, diving in from the one-yard line with about five minutes left to seal the victory for the Steelers. Therefore, in the modern age, like childbirth, the possibility of leaving one's children stranded might fall into the category of "acceptable excuses" for the premature exodus from a sporting event. A death in the family still might be another matter. I believe the Catholic term associated with this situation comes from the Latin, *memento mori*, loosely translated as "death comes to us all." So, in those cases, sit tight. Certainly, no one is going anywhere.

Growing up, we all had opinions of each other's parents. Overwhelmingly, however, in my circle of friends these opinions were mostly positive. Given the relatively light contact with each other's elders, it is fair to say that some parents were, at times, strict, and at other times cool. Sometimes, they would put a damper on things, but usually they were all very nice. This goes especially for the mothers who, looking back, put up with a lot of our shit.

I recall one instance when, after either playing football, baseball, or boxing at my friend Willie's house, the gang raided his kitchen and started devouring a pot of meatballs that was warming on the stove and was slated for dinner that night. I don't know what Willie's family ended up eating that day, but I can say, unequivocally, it wasn't meatballs. However, despite our midafternoon incursion to ward off starvation, there were no repercussions that I can recall.

All in all, we looked up to each other's parents—good people that were stuck in the unenviable positions of raising, well, us. But that September night at Shea was different. That was the first and perhaps only time that a friend's parent pulled what could only be classified as a "dick move."

The Pirates, having been shut out for four innings and down three to one after five, began to claw their way back. By the seventh inning stretch, they had tied the game 3-3. In the top of the eighth, with one out and the bases empty, Willie Stargell smashed a home run to center field giving the Bucs their first lead of the game, 4-3. My emotions that night had traveled from bored, to disappointed, to now excited. A crescendo was now building, one where, with the Phillies idle, the Pirates would only be three and one-half games back with thirteen left to play. Then, the unthinkable happened.

The Mets were dispatched in the bottom of the eighth by Kent Tekulve, the Pirates reliable right-handed, submarine-style reliever that had come on to blank the Mets after starter John Candelaria was pulled for a pinch hitter in the top of the seventh. As the organ music began between the eighth and ninth innings, the Pirates sat one inning away from vanquishing the Mets, splitting the series, and inching closer to the first-place Phils. Just then, I uttered the following words to my friend. I remember them as clearly as if it were yesterday: "See, this is why I never leave games early." Just then, my world, or better said, my world as a teenage Pirates fan, came crumbling down. "OK, let's go," said Mr. Dumont. With my mouth agape and frozen in my seat, he continued, "I want to beat the traffic."

There I sat, helpless in the back seat of Mr. Dumont's car as the Pirates collapsed in the bottom of the ninth when Lee Mazilli, with two out and one on, smacked a game-winning, walk-off homer off of Tekulve.

Six days later, by the end of play on September 26, 1976, the Pirates had slid to an insurmountable eight and a half games back with only five games to play. I was there for the Pirates' last chance at the NL East title before this fall from grace. But rather than sitting in the stands and dying with my team in person, I had to listen to it on the radio while staring out the window onto the Van Wyck Expressway.

Chapter 7
Ron Shanklin and the Feast of the Immaculate Reception

In September of 1972, not long after that first Pirates game at Three Rivers, my Aunt Aggie sent me a present for my eleventh birthday. It was a black Pittsburgh Steelers home jersey bearing the number "25," and with the name "Bellano" ironed on across the back shoulders in gold felt letters. However, while I could tell immediately it wasn't a "real" Steelers jersey, it was not a complete knock-off either. It had gold stripes on the arms that were not separated by white stripes, and the numbers on the front, back, and shoulders were gold, not white, like the uniform that was adopted by the organization in 1969, and which have essentially remained unchanged through the present day.

Looking back on it, Aunt Aggie's gift was, in fact, the home jersey that the Steelers wore from 1962 until 1965 and that reappeared when the NFL started to allow teams to don throwback uniforms at limited times during the season. To be more concise, my birthday present was the uniform that originally was accompanied by a yellow-colored helmet and, later, was worn when the team adopted the black helmet that is still in use today. To be clear, it was not the hideous "bumble bee," 1934 throwback uniform that makes the Steelers look like Mississippi chain gang escapees from the movie *O Brother, Where Art Thou?* Nor was it the "Batman" jersey that was worn in 1966–1968. In any event, Aunt Aggie's gesture was greatly appreciated. From a woman of very limited means, it became a beloved item of clothing that I wore until it nearly disintegrated.

Notwithstanding the name "Bellano" across the shoulders, at the time number twenty-five was worn by wide receiver Ron Shanklin. Shanklin was a solid, reliable pass catcher drafted by the Steelers in 1970. He led or was tied for the team lead in receptions from 1970 to 1973 and led in touchdowns in all of those years except 1972 when he was second.

However, as my coming of age as a Steelers fan did not occur until 1972, and the offense was primarily organized around the running game, I really didn't notice him or know who he was. As an illustration, in 1972 the Steelers ran the ball 497 times for 2,520 yards. Meanwhile, the Black and Gold's passing attack yielded only 1,958 yards in 156 attempts, a laughable tally by today's standards, but par for the course back then.

One must remember, the Forgettable Decade was an era in football where defense and running games were still paramount. On the defensive side of the ball, in addition to the Steel Curtain, the NFL boasted Minnesota's Purple People Eaters, the Rams' Fearsome Foursome, Dallas's Doomsday, and Miami's No Name.

While high-flying passing games had been introduced as a result of the AFL merger and were starting to be adopted by teams as a complement to the running game, in large part the NFL offensive philosophy of the day still had, at its core, "three yards and a cloud of dust."

Shanklin did garner a championship ring from being on the 1974 roster, the team that went on to win Super Bowl IX, but with the arrival of both Lynn Swann and John Stallworth that year, number twenty-five was reduced to nineteen receptions during the season and only one touchdown. Shanklin did not have a reception in Super Bowl IX, and by 1975, he was gone from the Steel City.

When that birthday present arrived in the mail in the late summer of 1972, it was not yet a fait accompli that the Steelers would be my team, as my father was not a huge football fan and he did not instill in me the same reverence of the sport as he had with regard to baseball and the Yankees. Also, baseball was my game. It was the sport I loved to play. At the time, when I grew up I wanted to be Bobby Murcer, not Bart Starr—I didn't even know who Bart Starr was.

However, I knew who Joe Namath was. The Jets' upset victory over the Baltimore Colts in Super Bowl III resonated so loudly through the New York metropolitan area that for someone seeking to expose themselves to football fandom, it was natural that the Jets would appear first on my radar screen. So, why didn't the Jets become the team for which I developed an obsessive love-hate relationship?

As I said, my interest in football developed later than that of baseball. And so, even with the Jets' historic Super Bowl win, in terms of football, my mind and heart were still in their formative stage. I do remember, quite vividly, listening to, not watching, the 1969 Jets divisional playoff game against the Kansas City Chiefs on a radio that sat on top of the buffet in our dining room. I can recall wanting the Jets to win and being bummed when they didn't, particularly when they couldn't get the ball in the end zone on two separate tries inside the five-yard line. This pair of futile exercises only resulted in three points and would turn out to be a metaphor for all Jets seasons to come. The Chiefs would go on to win Super Bowl IV, and the Jets would go on to descend into depths of hell for the remainder of the decade. Such was the end of my dalliance with the Jets. From then on, I liked them, but love was not in the cards.

Being a New Yorker, a town that has two professional teams in each of the four major sports, one is almost required to choose one team over another and announce, at an early age, a preference for one. It is, therefore, fair to say that, in the context of pro football, my "New York team" will always be the Jets, even though they played at Shea, home of the much-despised Mets.

In addition to the Jets' brief courtship with success, in those early days, there were other forces at work competing for my pigskin admiration. The aforementioned Vin Morelli from my Bat Day experience was a Green Bay Packers fan. Obviously, he had been introduced to football at an earlier age than I, and latched on to the Pack as a five- or six-year-old when they were winning three consecutive NFL championships, including the first two Super Bowls. Perhaps, more likely, his vegetable head dad was a Green Bay fan and passed on the mantle to little Vinny. Furthermore, contributing to the effects of Morelli's charismatic influence, another close friend of mine from the Saint Eugene's era, Joey Floyd, was so much of a devout Packers fan that he wore green suede Puma sneakers with yellow laces. "Puma suedes" were all the rage in the late grammar school years, and kids would buy the sneakers with colors as close to their team colors that one could get. Finally, Green Bay was also having success that fall, ultimately winning their conference's Central Division title in 1972 and making the playoffs. But, then again, so did the Steelers.

Despite these momentary distractions by devotees of the Badger State's professional football franchise, by December any internal struggle that may have existed was quashed forever, and my allegiance to the Steelers would be perpetually entrenched. As they say, blood is thicker than water, or, in this case, cheese. As a result of the Steelers jersey that Aunt Aggie had sent me along with my previously established connection to the Pirates and the Steel City, it became clear that, for me, any team that had a secondary uniform color of gold would forever only be coupled with the color black, not dark green. As the weeks unfolded, it wouldn't be long until I would be donning my own pair of Puma suedes, gold with a black stripe and black laces.

Because of the previously mentioned NFL blackout rules during that time, if a team in the local market had not sold out their game, it was not televised. Instead, the hometown fans would get intermittent doses of a smattering of other teams in the league. This was important as I was able to see the occasional Steelers game that fall because the Jets were so bad. Again, Giants fans had to suffer through what seemed like weekly doses of the Dallas Cowboys as, apparently, Giants games were rarely sold out in the '70s.

Of course, blackout rules or no blackout rules, playoff games were always televised. And while I had already crossed the Rubicon, really the Monongahela River, in terms of my pigskin allegiance, the die was formally cast on December 23, 1972, as the 10-3-1 Oakland Raiders brought their miserable silver and black carcasses into Three Rivers Stadium to face off against my 11-3 Steelers in the divisional round of the AFC playoffs.

Leading up to the game, I had already developed a significant animus for the Raiders going back to 1968 as a result of both the infamous Heidi Game and that year's AFC championship game against the Jets. The hirsute Raiders were a cocky and dirty squad. I could say they were dirty in the sense of being unkempt, but, then again, it was the '70s. Rather, they were dirty in the way gang bangers, cartel hit squads, or Mafia button men are. In my mind, there is a big difference between tough and dirty. The Steelers were tough. The Raiders were dirty. They were the antithesis of the clean-cut, prissy, holier-than-thou Cowboys. Despite this dichotomy in appearance, I fucking hated both teams.

There was much excitement and anticipation surrounding the game as the Raiders had been a perennial powerhouse, representing the AFL in Super Bowl II and appearing in the conference's championship game from 1967 through 1970. On the other hand, the Steelers were making their first playoff appearance since 490 B.C. when the Greeks defeated the Persians at the Battle of Marathon. Actually, it was 1947. That year, the Steelers played in the team's first and only prior playoff game and were unceremoniously whooped, 21-0, by their cross-state rivals, the Philadelphia Eagles.

The game lined up as a classic battle of NFL heavyweights, one proven and established, the other untested but on the ascent. The question on everyone's mind was whether the game would represent a passing of the torch or a reinforcement of the status quo. Further underscoring what was likely going to be a close, hard-fought battle was the fact that both the Steelers and Raiders were good at the same things: (1) stopping the rush, (2) putting pressure on the quarterback to disrupt the passing game, (3) running the ball, and (4) beating the shit out of each other.

On that December day, the Mel Blount Rule, prohibiting contact with wide receivers beyond five yards of the line of scrimmage, had not come into play yet. Rules for or against "the tuck," "in the grasp," and "hitting a defenseless player," while they may have been on the books in some form, did not seem to be enforced. In the 1970s, the term "incidental contact" was not in the NFL nomenclature.

For purposes of illustration of what the two teams were in store for that day, we can turn to today's *NFL Rulebook*, Article 11, which contains referee guidance for situations that involve roughing the passer and contrast it to those of the 1970s. Below are some selective excerpts from the current rules:

> *a) Roughing will be called if, in the Referee's judgment, a pass rusher clearly should have known that the ball had already left the passer's hand before contact was made; pass rushers are responsible for being aware of the position of the ball in passing situations...[and the pass rusher shall] attempt to avoid contact and must not continue to "drive through" or otherwise forcibly contact the passer...*

> *b) When tackling a passer who is in a defenseless posture...a defensive player must not unnecessarily or violently throw him down or land*

> *on top of him with all or most of the defender's weight. Instead, the defensive player must strive to…brace his fall with his arms to avoid landing on the quarterback with all or most of his body weight… Note: …a standard of strict liability applies for any contact against a passer, irrespective of any acts by the passer, such as ducking his head or curling up his body in anticipation of contact.*

Black's Law Dictionary defines strict liability, in part, as "liability that does not depend on actual negligence or intent to harm, but that is based on the breach of an absolute duty to make something safe." This explains the number of incredulous defensive players and bewildered fans when flags are thrown on too many given Sundays because they did not realize, at 250-plus pounds and the ability to run a 4.6 forty, defensive players had an absolute duty to keep opposing quarterbacks safe. On the other hand, having watched many, many games throughout the Forgettable Decade, I feel it unnecessary to go back and dig up the 1970s version of the *NFL Rulebook*. Rather, I thought it best to take a crack at it and try and paraphrase my interpretation of the roughing the passer rule at the time: "Roughing the passer shall be called upon a pass rusher in the event the passer's head, or any limb, is severed from the passer's body. Contact with a passer after he has come off the field and is seated on his team's sideline bench shall also constitute a penalty. Contact with a passer in the stadium parking lot or a bar after the game shall fall under the jurisdiction of local law enforcement and is outside the purview of the referee…"

As far as the Steelers being up and coming, their 11-3 record spoke for itself. However, the team's ascendency into an AFC divisional round playoff game was rather meteoric, given that from 1968 to 1971 the Steelers compiled a typically dismal record of 14-41-1. But their 1972 success was not *solely* due to high draft picks that bore fruit after, save a handful of seasons, forty-two years of below .500 records. Rather, in 1969, two high-pressure systems, one from the coaching ranks and the other from the college draft, collided to create a perfect squall (the perfect storm would come in 1974).

In January of 1969, owner Art Rooney, who had weathered the trials and tribulations of four decades of disappointment and frustration, hired former San Diego Chargers defensive coordinator and current Baltimore Colts defensive co-coordinator Chuck Noll. In Baltimore, Noll worked under the legendary Don Shula and alongside future Miami Dolphins defensive guru Bill Arnsparger.

The stoic, disciplinarian Noll, aided by a decade of shitty seasons that yielded those high draft picks, got to work immediately. In 1969, with the assistance of sports journalist turned uber-scout, Bill Nunn, the Steelers picked fourth overall and took defensive tackle and future Hall of Famer "Mean" Joe Greene out of North Texas State. In the same draft but nine rounds later, the Rooneys and Noll picked L. C. Greenwood, defensive end from Arkansas Pine Bluff, who by the way should be in the Hall of Fame, but isn't. Both men, especially Greene, would be the building blocks of what came to be known as the "Steel Curtain" defense, the most formidable, dominant defense of the Forgettable Decade. Some, like me, would argue of all time.

Despite the successful draft of 1969, the Steelers had another horrid season in the win-loss column, finishing the year 1-13. This did, however, give the Steelers the number one overall pick in the 1970 draft. This time the Rooney-Noll brain trust chose a quarterback, Terry Bradshaw, out of Louisiana Tech University, another future Hall of Famer. The first pick in the third round belonged to the Steelers, and they chose Southern University cornerback and future Hall of Famer Mel Blount. Ron Shanklin was the first pick in the second round that year. The 1970 Steelers improved slightly, finishing the season with five wins against nine losses.

In 1971, the Steelers took Penn State linebacker and future Hall of Famer Jack Ham. (Do you see a pattern emerging?) With two picks in the fourth round, the Black and Gold front office chose defensive end

Dwight White, L. C. Greenwood's bookend on the Steel Curtain, and offensive lineman Gerry Mullins. All three, Ham, White, and Mullins, would play the balance of the decade in Black and Gold and be major contributors to the four world championships that lay ahead. Back in the 1971 first round, the Steelers drafted Frank Lewis, a solid, dependable receiver out of Grambling that would be Ron Shanklin's receiver corps tandem mate. I use the benign term "dependable" here as a compliment. In the running back–centric seventies, a pair of dependable possession receivers was a necessary complement to the run game.

Despite the bevy of talent moving into the locker room, the young players were still raw and unformed. Something was missing in order for Noll and Rooney to make progress on the jigsaw puzzle for victory that was emptied onto the Steel City's dining room table in 1969. After another mediocre season in 1971, the Steelers, with the thirteenth pick in the 1972 draft, selected Franco Harris, a six-foot-two, 230-pound running back from Penn State and, yes, a future Hall of Famer.

In his rookie season, Harris would rush for over one thousand yards, only the second Steeler to ever do so and the first since John Henry Johnson, nearly a decade earlier. He was named NFL Rookie of the Year by the Associated Press, the Pro Football Writers of America, and the *Sporting News.* Like a random beaker of chemicals that gets spilled into another lab experiment and transforms one substance into another, Franco Harris sparked a reaction in the Steelers that metamorphosed a team that had averaged ten losses a year over the last four years into a 11-3 division winner with a home field playoff berth and the team's first in a quarter of a century.

On game day, Three Rivers Stadium was lined with banners, hand painted on sheets by the Steelers faithful. Each player, it seemed, had their own rooting section. Kicker Roy Gerela had "Gerela's Gorillas." There were "Count Fuqua's Foreign Legion," supporting fullback John "Frenchy" Fuqua; "Joe Greene's Polish Armed Forces, Green Babushka 75"; "Russel's Raiders"; and of course, "Franco's Italian Army." Linebacker Jack Ham must have been a favorite among my Slovak sistren and brethren in the region as his sign read, "Jack Ham, Dobre Shunka," which translates from Slovak as "Jack Ham, Good Ham."

Game-time temperature was unseasonably mild for the day before Christmas Eve in Pittsburgh, an almost balmy forty-two degrees. To contrast, fifty years and a day after the game, I attended the golden anniversary of the Immaculate Reception and what turned out to be a memorial game for Franco Harris, who had passed away suddenly only days earlier. The temperature at game time had climbed from subzero temps during the day to about nine degrees, but a windchill brought with it the feel of an Antarctic expedition. And at some point during the game, it started to snow again. Back to the '72 game, the Steelers were two-point favorites, which in a time where defense, field position, and the kicking game were paramount, the spread was basically a push.

As expected, from the opening kickoff these two evenly matched teams in talent and record immediately locked into a defensive stalemate that culminated with a scoreless first half. The only whiff of a possible score was a fifty-two-yard field goal attempt by Roy Gerela that fell pathetically short. Illustrative of overwhelming defensive dominance, during the contest the two teams combined for three interceptions, two lost fumbles, and seven quarterback sacks. Fortunately, by game's end, those numbers broke in the Steelers' favor. Astonishingly, only three penalties for twenty yards were called on both teams. We can assume, therefore, that the refs, as the saying goes, let them play.

This edge-of-your-seat, nail-biting contest would continue throughout the first fifty-six minutes of the game. By the late fourth quarter, the Steel Curtain was pitching a shutout and the Raiders had grudgingly yielded two field goals, leaving my team with a tenuous six-point lead with about four minutes to play. This situation, where the Steelers were ahead but had not put the game away, would be a trend that continues up to the present day, much to the chagrin of the Pittsburgh faithful. Whether ending in a win or a loss, Steelers games, until the final whistle, usually involve stress, trauma, and near cardiac arrest.

After the second Gerela field goal and subsequent touchback, the Raiders got to work at their own twenty-yard line with 3:36 left in the contest.

During the course of the game, Raiders quarterback and "Mad Bomber" Daryle Lamonica had been ineffective all day, throwing two interceptions to Steelers defenders. Late in the third quarter, the veteran quarterback was replaced with southpaw Kenny "the Snake" Stabler, who had been getting limited time over his two-year, nascent career but was clearly being groomed as the heir apparent to Lamonica.

In eleven plays, aided by a fourth-down conversion and a Steelers offside penalty, Stabler drove the Raiders fifty yards to the Pittsburgh thirty. With my young blood pressure already rising to almost stroke proportions, in a blink of an eye, my world came to what I thought was a traumatic end.

On first and ten, Stabler looked downfield to move the Oakland offense closer to the goal line. Raiders receivers flooded the right side of the field, and the Steelers defense followed. Overrunning the play, the Steel Curtain vacated the entire left side of the field, allowing the Snake to slither thirty yards into the end zone. When veteran and relic kicker/ quarterback George Blanda added the extra point with only 1:13 left, Oakland led 7 to 6.

The emotional roller coaster I experienced from the last Gerela field goal through that Oakland scoring drive made Rye Playland's Dragon Coaster look like a kiddie ride. First euphoria, then nervousness, then anticipation, then apprehension, and finally, devastation. After leading for fifty-eight minutes and forty-seven seconds, I began preparing myself for the worst. I dropped to my knees, tanto at the ready. I did not curse my God, as I would in the case of a baseball rainout. Instead, I was pre-pared to meet my maker via hara-kiri.

An alternative glimmer of hope lay in the possibility that, by some miracle, the Steelers could move the ball with just over a minute re-maining against the obstinate Raiders defense that would be sitting back anticipating a drive composed solely of passes. If there was one ray of sunshine that peaked through the overcast Three Rivers Stadium sky, it was that the Steelers only needed a field goal, not a touchdown, to snatch victory from the jaws of defeat.

While Roy Gerela had been almost perfect on extra points and a solid seventeen for nineteen on field goals from twenty-nine yards or less in 1972, longer field goals were another matter. Things got much more dicey for the Pittsburgh placekicker farther out as he was only eleven for twenty-two beyond thirty yards.

Now, after the ensuing kickoff and touchback, with the ball at their own twenty, the Steelers would need to drive fifty or sixty yards in order to have a legitimate field goal attempt and serious chance at victory (in 1972 NFL goalposts were still on the goal line and wouldn't be moved to the back of the end zone until 1974).

Dramatic cannot sufficiently describe the series of events that un-folded during that last Steelers drive. Justice can only be done with a recount of the play-by-play:

- 1st and 10 at the Pittsburgh 20; Bradshaw pass complete to Har-ris to the Pittsburgh 29; 56 seconds remaining.
- 2nd and 1 at the Pittsburgh 29; Bradshaw pass complete to Fuqua to the Pittsburgh 40; Pittsburgh calls timeout with 37 seconds remaining.
- 1st and 10 at the Pittsburgh 40; Bradshaw pass intended for Mc-Makin, broken up by Jack Tatum; 31 seconds remaining.
- 2nd and 10 at the Pittsburgh 40; Bradshaw pass intended for Shanklin, broken up by George Atkinson; 26 seconds remaining.

- 3rd and 10 at the Pittsburgh 40; Bradshaw pass intended for Mc-Makin, broken up by Jack Tatum; 22 seconds remaining.
- 4th and 10 at the Pittsburgh 40; under heavy pressure, Bradshaw scrambles; pass intended for Fuqua, broken up by Jack Tatum; 5 seconds remaining.

But, as we all know, that's not the end of the story.

As the Raiders defenders and sidelines began jumping in celebration, a Black and Gold specter, wearing number thirty-two, picked the deflected ball out of the air at the Oakland forty-two and raced down the sideline into the end zone.

What ensued next was chaos. Steelers fans poured onto the field. The Steelers ran to the end zone to join the celebration. The Raiders stood frozen in shock and disbelief. I was mimicking both the Steelers and their fans jumping and rolling around on my playroom floor.

It took what seemed like an eternity for the referees to sort out the play, clear the field, and set up for Gerela's extra point. Once the pandemonium subsided, a squibbed kick touchback followed by an unsuccessful, desperation pass by Stabler drained the final seconds off the clock. The Steelers were victorious and had earned a place in next week's AFC championship game, all on the wings of a play, soon to be named the "Immaculate Reception," and which would be voted the greatest play in NFL history by the NFL Network.

I will not get into a debate on the half-century-old whining of Raiders fans that still believe that Fuqua, and only Fuqua, running horizontally on a crossing pattern across the middle somehow touched the ball and sent it ricocheting backward seven yards into Franco's outstretched arms, therefore, making it an illegal catch. The pass definitely hit Tatum. It may have hit Fuqua and Tatum. If it did, it's a catch. Get over it.

To reemphasize how close the game was, the statistics tell a compelling story. The Raiders outrushed the Steelers by 30 yards. The teams were tied with 108 yards each before Stabler's 30-yard jaunt into the end zone with just over a minute left.

At the snap on the 4th and 10 play before the 60-yard Immaculate Reception, the Steelers had a slight edge in the passing game 115 yards to Oakland's 102. As with the Stabler scramble, one play made the difference. More than a third of the two teams' combined total offensive output took place in the last three and a half minutes of the game. Almost a quarter occurred in the last minute and a half.

That game and its dramatic and, according to the Raiders, controversial outcome, concluded by one of the most bizarre plays in not only NFL but sports history, became the genesis of an intense, hard-fought, sometimes brutal rivalry between the Steelers and Raiders that would last most of the decade. The two franchises would play out these conflicts on the largest of stages.

Amplifying what would become one of the NFL's most intense rivalries, of the ten AFC championship games played from 1970 until the end of the 1979 season, either the Raiders or the Steelers stood on the sideline in all but one, 1971. In three of those contests, the two teams faced off against each other, 1974 through 1976. The two teams would also appear in five Super Bowls during the Forgettable Decade, knocking helmets with each other a total of five times in the postseason.

Oh, by the way, the first teammate to greet Franco Harris in the end zone after the Immaculate Reception? Number twenty-five, Ron Shanklin.

Larry Fuckin' Seiple and the Agony of Defeat

Due to a quirk in the 1972 NFL playoff schedule where the home field was determined by divisional rotation, not best record, the following week the Steelers played host to the defending AFC champions and currently undefeated Miami Dolphins.

If anticipation was high for the Raiders game, it was off the charts for the AFC championship matchup. It was one thing to make the playoffs. It was another to have defeated the hated Raiders, especially on such a historic play. But now, the Steelers stood at the precipice of being in the Super Bowl. Once again, my vital signs monitor was beeping and flashing.

If the temperature in the Steel City was balmy for the Raiders game, it was downright tropical for the Dolphin contest. With the mercury in the sixties for most of the game, weather played into the Dolphins' hands and negated any cold weather advantage that might have accompanied the NFL's idiosyncratic home field playoff rule.

From the kickoff, things looked good. On the Dolphins' first possession, safety Glen Edwards picked off a pass from Miami's dinosauric quarterback Earl Morrell and ran the ball back into Miami territory. The ensuing drive was textbook Steelers, three yards and a cloud of artificial turf. Nine running plays later, seven by Franco Harris, Pittsburgh was at the three-yard line.

On third and two, Terry Bradshaw rolled left and ran a quarterback option, although I don't think he ever considered passing the ball. Almost immediately, he tucked the ball in and headed for the end zone. At the two-yard line, he was met by Dolphin defensive back Jake Scott, who, as they say in the business, laid the wood to Bradshaw, who hit the unforgiving turf field on his right shoulder. The Pittsburgh quarterback coughed up the ball. Luckily for the Steelers, it spewed forward and offensive lineman Gerry Mullins fell on the ball for a Pittsburgh touchdown.

Fifty thousand–plus Pittsburgh fans rejoiced. Tens of thousands of TV viewers, including me, cheered. Steelers' players on the field and sidelines celebrated. Except one. After the play, and unnoticeable to most, Terry Bradshaw lay prone near the goal line. Eventually helped off the field with an apparent injured right shoulder (his throwing arm) as a result of the Scott hit, and with diagnosis pending, elation, still the prominent emotion among the fans, was now tempered by concern.

Bradshaw returned, however, for one series after the injury, but it was clear the trauma was affecting his ability to throw, or even play at all. The damage to Bradshaw's shoulder would send him to the sidelines for an indefinite period of time. The Steelers, leading 7-0, would now have to look to their backup quarterback, Terry Hanratty, to guide the team's championship effort.

Hanratty was a product of western Pennsylvania, an area that spawned many Hall of Fame quarterbacks, including Johnny Unitas, Joe Montana, Dan Marino, and Jim Kelly. Hanratty, however, would not be joining that list anytime soon.

Hanratty was a former college star at Notre Dame and had led the Fighting Irish to the national championship in 1966. In 1968, he finished third in the Heisman Trophy voting, about a mile behind University of Southern California (USC) standout Orenthal J. Simpson. In 1969, he was drafted by the Steelers in the second round, right behind Mean Joe Greene, and given the chance to play, rotating the quarterback duties with journeyman Dick Shiner, who had landed in Pittsburgh for the 1968–1969 seasons. As mentioned above, the Steelers finished 1-13 in 1969 and immediately went to the draft looking for another quarterback, Bradshaw, as the first overall pick in 1970. From that point on, Hanratty would be in a backup role, with his snaps diminishing precipitously between 1970 and 1975, his last year with the franchise. The one exception was 1973 where Bradshaw lost multiple weeks due to a separated shoulder.

In any event, with the Pittsburgh starter now out of the game, Hanratty trotted out on the field, having only limited playing time under his belt, making spot appearances in only seven games in 1972, and attempting only four passes, two of which were completed for a total of twenty-three yards.

As he entered the game and stood under center, his ample black hair and thick dark mustache stood in stark contrast to the blond Bradshaw. With the season and the AFC championship on the line, Hanratty took the helm looking like a cross between Super Mario in an undersized football helmet and Bill "the Butcher" Cutting, the character played by Daniel Day-Lewis in Martin Scorsese's *Gangs of New York*, that is, if Cutting had been an Irish immigrant rather than a terrorizer of them. Although, like Cutting, due to his limited play during the season, Hanratty came into the championship game as a bit of a Know-Nothing.

Given that the first rule of being a backup quarterback in such a critical spot is, "Don't fuck things up!" Hanratty was going to be on a short leash. But it wasn't a mistake due to Hanratty's lack of playing time that would turn things around in the first half.

On their second possession after the Pittsburgh touchdown and as the second quarter began, Miami was held short of another first down. Lining up on his own thirty-five yard line, Dolphins punter Larry Seiple saw that the Steelers' punt team had completely abandoned the rush to set up for the return. Seeing a gap the width and length of the Florida Intracoastal, he took off with the ball. By the time the Steelers' woke up and got their act together, Larry fuckin' Seiple, as he would forever be known, had maneuvered himself down to the Pittsburgh twelve.

Two plays later, the Dolphins were in the end zone and the game was tied at seven points apiece. With Noll running a conservative offense under Hanratty's direction, and the Steel Curtain dominating on defense, the two teams continued to trade punts and played out the rest of the first half to a deadlock.

As Pittsburgh received the second-half kickoff, there was one, only one, semishining moment with Hanratty at the helm. On their first possession of the third quarter, aided by a couple of impressive passes and strong running by Franco Harris and Frenchy Fuqua, the Steelers moved the ball down to the Miami eight. The drive stalled there, however, and the Steelers had to settle for a field goal and a precarious 10-7 lead.

Then, for the second time in as many weeks, Steelers' opponents pulled their starting quarterback. Last week it was Stabler for Lamonica that almost led to disaster. This week it was veteran Earl Morrell being replaced by Bob Greise, who was the regular Dolphins starter but who had been hampered by injuries all season.

Like Stabler the week before, Griese rallied the Dolphins on an eighty-yard drive, maneuvering Miami downfield until the Steelers defense, now spending an inordinate time on the field, could not stop their opponents on a goal line stand. Toward the end of the drive, Don Shula's team opted to go on fourth and a half yard, rather than taking a game-tying field goal. The gamble was successful, and two plays later the Dolphins were once again in the end zone. And so, for the first time in the game, with three and a half minutes left in the third quarter, Miami took the lead. Dolphins 14, Steelers 10.

Preston Pearson's runback after the Dolphin touchdown put the Steelers in good field position near midfield. But the dysfunctional Bradshaw-less offense continued to struggle. The best the offense could do was advance to the Miami forty. This set up a forty-eight-yard field goal attempt by Roy Gerela.

The kick was blocked, giving Miami the ball in Steelers territory with under fourteen minutes left in the game. Griese would continue to rally the Dolphins, moving them again inside the Steelers' five on a drive that seemed to last an eternity and would ultimately eat up an additional six and a half minutes. Once again, the Steel Curtain stiffened and, once again, Miami was faced with a fourth down and short decision. Like before, Shula went for it on fourth down and was successful again. As with the Dolphins' last drive, two plays after the conversion, running back Jim Kick squirted into the end zone. Dolphins 21, Steelers 10.

On the ensuing drive, Pittsburgh received their own spark as Bradshaw returned to the game behind center with just over seven minutes to play. Like Lazarus rising from the dead, Bradshaw quickly drove the entombed Steelers offense down the field on only five plays, capped by a one-handed, leaping grab by backup wide receiver Al Young, on what looked like an overthrown pass. Young's circus catch cut the Miami lead to four. Dolphins 21, Steelers 17.

It is important to mention Don Shula's aggressiveness during the possessions that led to Miami's last two scores. Perhaps, it is what great teams that end up going undefeated do. Despite the stinginess of the Steel Curtain on prior plays near the goal line, Shula called for two fourth-down conversions at critical times on that championship Sunday (Miami actually did it three times, but the two touchdowns were where it counted most). Going for a pair of fourth and less-than-a-yard conversions inside the Steelers' five-yard line was the difference between the Dolphins being on top 21-10 and a 17-16 or 17-13 Steelers lead after Bradshaw's return. I do not believe, given the same situation, that the conservative Chuck Noll would have done the same thing. Certainly not twice.

Although the Steel Curtain would force a three and out on Miami's next possession, time and a less than 100 percent Bradshaw were factors that did not portend well for a Steelers comeback. But with three minutes and twenty-one seconds remaining, there was hope, albeit, perhaps, only in the form of diehard fan optimism.

However, on the first play, Bradshaw was sacked for nine yards. The Steelers quarterback's second-down pass fell incomplete. On the next play, anything approaching a Steelers new life would quickly turn from hope to anticipation to calamity. Bradshaw's third and nineteen pass was thrown short over the middle toward a sea of white jerseys and into the arms of Dolphins middle linebacker Nick Buoniconti.

The resulting Miami drive, again starting in Pittsburgh territory, took almost two minutes, truncated by Steelers timeouts. It ended with another attempted fourth-down conversion by Shula, this time opting out of the field goal and a seven-point lead in an effort to run out the clock. But the Steel Curtain rose up one last time and stopped fullback Larry Csonka for a loss, leaving the Steelers with ninety yards and thirty-nine seconds to attempt another miracle finish. However, nothing immaculate was in the cards for the Black and Gold this championship Sunday. After a nine-yard pass to Franco, Bradshaw was picked off for a second time, ending Steel City's fans' hopes and preserving Miami's undefeated season heading into the Super Bowl.

As if the loss to the Dolphins wasn't bad enough, later that very same day the world learned of the death of Pirates great Roberto Clemente. As mentioned earlier, Clemente died in a plane crash while on a humanitarian mission for earthquake victims in Nicaragua.

And so, in the space of eight days I experienced emotions spanning the highest exhilaration to the inconsolable depths of depression. I had climbed to the summit of Everest and then, within a week and a day, was flung down to the deepest depths of the Mariana Trench. I was crushed, but from now on I was all in. I was hooked. I was a Steelers fan.

Chapter 8

Say It Ain't So, George!

October 23, 1974, while generally nondescript in the vast chronology of human history, for me, had started out by all indications to be a good day. Actually, a day better than most. As a student at Saint Eugene's Catholic Elementary School, Wednesdays meant a shortened day with a 1:00 p.m. dismissal. The reason for the school's early hump day departure was due to the fact that the classrooms and teachers had to get ready for taking in public school children that would wander in after their school day for religious instruction, formally known as the Confraternity of Christian Doctrine, or, more commonly, CCD.

As Catholic school students, we had a daily class in religion. The drumbeat of the catechism that reverberated in our heads and had been a part of our lives since first grade prepared us for any of the ritual obligations laid out by the Catholic Church. Therefore, when it was time, for example, to receive the sacraments of Penance (i.e., Confession), First Holy Communion, or Confirmation, we'd be more than ready.

The same could not be said for the public school heathens who, in order to prepare *thyselves* for the way of the Lord, had to spend their

Wednesday afternoons learning about Noah, Job, and Pontius Pilate. For us, however, those stories had become second nature, the equivalent of nursery rhymes or the ABC's in the secular world.

While I can't remember specifically, I was probably in a rather upbeat mood starting off the day. Leaving school early has that effect on most eighth graders. Also, as was the more recent custom, I was driven to school by my mother, who had recently gotten her driver's license a year or two earlier. The days of *schlogging* to the corner bus stop and waiting for the Royal Coach Lines school bus were over. A more convenient and a much cooler way to get to school had evolved, provided I was dropped off far enough away so my friends didn't see.

I must say, God bless my mother for taking me on this daily trek in our 1972 Ford Custom 500 that we had purchased used, but with very low mileage, from my father's cousin, a marketing executive with General Foods. If I remember correctly, it was one of their corporate vehicles, known in those days as a "company car" that became available. Uncle Mickey, knowing we were in the market for a car, offered the opportunity to my father. The Custom 500 was a metallic green supertanker of a car. In other words, a typical American family car of the era. Driving it on roads such as the Saw Mill, Bronx, or Hutchinson River Parkways could be stressful, like navigating the Exxon Valdez down a bobsled run. All in all, the Custom 500 was a great car. It ran well and never leaked oil like ol' Joe Hazelwood's ship. The Custom 500 had replaced our 1966 Buick LeSabre, a mere aircraft carrier-sized vehicle, which in turn had succeeded a 1958 Plymouth—either Fury or Belvedere. I have no memory of the Plymouth, just stories from my sisters about the vehicle's hideous gray and pink color; however, there is a photo of me as a toddler hanging out the back window of the sedan that must have only had Carnival cruise ship–like dimensions.

There were, however, two downsides to the car. First, it was purchased right around the time of the first Middle East oil embargo. While the Custom 500's performance specifications claim that the car got 20.1 miles per gallon on the highway and 16.7 miles per gallon in city driving, that is wishful thinking. Needless to say, by the time the second oil embargo came around in 1979, the Custom 500 had already been replaced by a slightly more fuel-efficient Ford Torino sedan, another "company car," this time purchased directly from my father's employer, the A&P.

Second, the massive, 70s green, gas-guzzling sedan only came equipped with an AM radio, greatly diminishing the family's motorized listening options. Basically, AM listeners in the New York metropolitan area were reduced to a handful of stations, mostly news and Top 40 music in mono. Mobile audiences would typically turn their dials to one of the following six stations: WNBC or WABC for the morning drive and the aforementioned Top 40 hits. For New York metro area news and weather, there was either WINS, better known as "1010Wins," or its chief competitor, WCBS, known as "WCBS Eight Eighty." In the afternoons and evenings, one could wander over to WMCA that carried Yankees games for most of the 1970s. More rarely, one might find themselves down the dial to 1050 WHN, the country music station, to perhaps pick up an Elvis, Eagles, or Linda Ronstadt tune (as if "Blue Bayou" wasn't saturating the other stations).

In the morning drive, WABC featured "Cousin Brucie," Bruce Morrow, and WNBC, where our dial was normally set for school commutes, boasted Imus in the Morning, the original shock jock of the morning drive time. It was here, on this fifty-thousand-watt mega station that darkness descended over my horizon on that October morning. Emanating through the car speakers during the news/sportscast of Imus's longtime right-hand man, Charles McCord, came the devastating news.

And so, on that October day in 1974 we were off for the daily trek to school. On a typical morning, we'd pull out of our driveway onto Candlewood Drive, then a left onto Pembrooke Drive, followed by another left on Mountaindale Road. At a traffic light, we would make a third left on Tuckahoe Road, a left, again, onto Central Avenue, a quick right up the hill at Seneca Avenue, and, finally, a right onto Massitoa Road and into Saint Eugene's parking lot. But, on that fateful day, our morning commute took a cataclysmic turn.

Born in 1961, I do not remember where I was when John F. Kennedy was shot. Similarly, with the Bobby Kennedy and Martin Luther King Jr. assassinations, I don't remember where I was but can make an educated guess. King, having been killed at about 6:00 p.m. on April 4, 1968, and Kennedy, gunned down just after midnight PST on June 5 of the same year, I would surmise that I was eating dinner (no TV allowed at the dinner table) and sleeping, respectively.

However, on October 23, 1974, I know exactly where I was, the final curve where Pembrooke Drive hits Mountaindale Road. Without doing a deep dive into the Imus in the Morning archives, I can, without hesitation, paraphrase McCord's words: "George Steinbrenner once said he wouldn't trade away Bobby Murcer for Yankee Stadium, but yesterday he traded him to the San Francisco Giants for Bobby Bonds."

Steinbrenner, who, with a group of investors, purchased the Yankees from CBS in January of 1973, had vowed to return the franchise to greatness and, with major league baseball poised at the dawn of free agency, promised to spare no expense in order to do so. The Yankees had not appeared in the World Series since losing back-to-back fall classics to Sandy Koufax's Dodgers in 1963 and Bob Gibson's Cardinals in 1964.

But for a thirteen-year-old, hearing that his boyhood idol, the player he tried to emulate on the Little League field, the Yankee he traveled to the Bronx to see and specifically root for, had just been banished to some faraway place was a gut punch, a betrayal of the first magnitude. For the teenage me, at the time, this ultimate betrayal was more devastating than being turned down for a date from a teenage crush.

When Murcer arrived in the Bronx, he was touted as the next Mickey Mantle, *his* boyhood idol. Like Mantle, he was from Oklahoma.

He had been signed by the same scout as the Mick. However, after joining the Yankees in 1965 and short stretches back and forth to the minors, Murcer was drafted in 1967 to serve a two-year stint in the US Army.

Also, like Mantle, he broke into the big leagues as a shortstop and later moved to his permanent position as the Yankees center fielder, a position that had previously been occupied by the likes of Mantle and the great Joe DiMaggio. Predating the Yankee Clipper was the lesser known Earle Combs, who patrolled Yankee Stadium's Death Valley in the 1920s and 1930s and was a member of the vaunted Murderer's Row that amassed multiple World Series titles. In 1969, Murcer had been given the opportunity to play in the same rarified air as Mantle, DiMaggio, and Combs.

Let's get one thing straight: Murcer was never Mickey Mantle. He was never going to be Mickey Mantle. But he was *my* Mickey Mantle, or at least my first Mantle, meaning my first sports idol. I remember hearing that Murcer had suffered a thumb injury, which he tried to relieve by taping a sponge to his bat. For a while, I copied the exercise, doing the same to my own Louisville Slugger. Like Murcer, I was a lefty batter (however, Murcer threw righty) and I mimicked his swing when I was at bat. In my first year as a Little Leaguer, I lobbied to play center field.

Ultimately, as is the nature of Little League games, especially in those fledging years, center field does not lend itself to a lot of action, and I was extremely bored playing the position. The next year, at my father's advice, I switched to first base, the position where I would spend the balance of my Little League and high school playing career, as well as into adulthood when age crept in and softball replaced baseball.

After returning from the military, Murcer's first two seasons in pinstripes were solid, not exceptional, certainly not Mantle-esque, but respectable. In 1969 and 1970, he batted a mediocre .259 and .251, respectively. During those two years, however, he drove in 160 runs and hit 49 home runs. His high number of strikeouts (204) over that time, perhaps, evidences the combined pressures of playing in the historic position of center field as the heir to the Mick, and being overaggressive while staring at the stadium's short right field porch. In his remaining four years as a Yankee, he settled down and averaged about one half the strikeouts per year than he did in 1969–1970.

1971 was the breakout year for Murcer. That season, he finished second in the American League in batting with a .331 average, hit 25 home runs, and was fourth in RBIs with 94. In 1972, Murcer's 33 home runs placed him second in the AL behind Chicago's Dick Allen and third in RBIs behind only sluggers Allen and John Mayberry. He finished that season with a .292 average.

Murcer was featured on the cover of the July 2, 1973, issue of *Sports Illustrated* with teammate Ron Bloomberg, the American League's first designated hitter, with the headline: "The Pride of the New Yankees." Murcer followed up the article with impressive numbers for 1973: .304 batting average, 22 homers, and batting in 95 runs. The Yankees, after languishing for almost a decade in the doldrums, were becoming interesting again. Along with fellow teammate and good friend Thurman Munson, who had captured AL Rookie of the Year honors in 1970, the guys in pinstripes prompted echoes of a reincarnation of the M&M Boys, the nickname given to Mantle and Roger Maris in 1961 as they chased Babe Ruth's single-season home run record.

Murcer was a perennial all-star who hit 20-plus homers with regularity and consistently flirted with the 100 RBI mark during his tenure with the team. Yankee Stadium's short right field porch, only 296 feet down the line in those days, was tailor-made for his swing.

In 1973, Murcer became only the third player in Bronx Bombers history to earn $100,000, joining Yankees greats Babe Ruth and Joe DiMaggio. At the start of that fateful 1974 season, Murcer's salary jumped to $120,000, becoming the highest-paid Yankees player ever.

However, renovations to Yankee Stadium during the 1974 and 1975 seasons forced the Bombers to be banished to Queens. This would turn out to be the beginning of the end of Murcer's tenure in the Bronx. During those two years, Murcer's offensive productivity noticeably declined while playing at the shithole that was Shea Stadium. While still driving in eighty-eight runs, he was limited to only ten homers, only two of which were hit at the New York metropolitan area's incarnation of Alcatraz on Flushing Bay.

And so, on that October morning, he was gone. Like Jesus being handed over to the Romans, the Judas, Steinbrenner, handed Bobby over to the Giants and sealed his fate.

Upon Murcer being traded to San Francisco, I faced my first fan crisis. Would my adoration for Bobby Murcer be stronger than my love of all things pinstripes? Would I take my anger out on George Steinbrenner and change allegiances by becoming a San Francisco Giants fan or, God forbid, start rooting for the Mets? The horror, the *horror*!

As it turned out, blood was thicker than water. Meaning, my father's instilling not only a love for the team but the traditions, history, and mystique of the Bronx Bombers as well, would prove too strong. I lived in New York. Most of my friends were Yankees fans, and I could watch or listen to the Yanks on TV or the radio whenever I wanted. Time would pass, and life as a Yankees fan proved exponentially more interesting than becoming a San Francisco Giants fan or just a Murcer fan.

Despite this first encounter with grief, I came to grips with the sadness and the anger. And, as we know, baseball is a game of redemption. You can strike out three times and still get the game-winning hit in the bottom of the ninth and be the hero. In the ensuing few years, the Yankees roster changed for the better and success came over the next few years. Murcer, therefore, became not forgotten but simply put on the back burner of my mind. The redemption of Bobby Ray Murcer would take almost five years to materialize. Yet, come it did, for one more fleeting moment in one of the most memorable Yankees games ever played.

Chapter 9
The Rise of the Steel Curtain—Super Bowls IX and X

Coming off the euphoric high of the Immaculate Reception and the subsequent low of the Dolphin loss in the championship game, the Steelers and I went into 1973 with tremendous optimism. From a general sports perspective, to date, the year had been a bust as the NFL season began. Since I didn't care much about basketball, the Knicks championship win over both the detested Celtics and the hated Lakers was nice, but I doubt it carried me more than a few days from a fan-elation perspective. Also, the '72–'73 school year was the aforementioned same-sex grade format with the pervert in chief, Tom McMann, at the helm.

In addition, the Yankees, who would be banished to Queens the following year as renovations would commence on the House That Ruth Built, finished fourth in the AL East in 1973. The Pirates did not fare much better, finishing third in their division. Both teams, as if to personally taunt me, ended the season two games under .500 at a lackluster 80-82.

As if this was not bad enough, the friggin' Mets won the NL East and beat the Reds for the pennant, something the Pirates would fail to do on three out of four occasions in the 1970s. While the Mets loss to the Oakland A's in the World Series brightened things up a bit, for the most part, I would have to rely on the Steelers to bring happiness to my otherwise pitiful fan experience. It did not happen.

Although the Steelers finished 10-4 that year, they were relegated to wild card status as the Cincinnati Bengals, inbred cousins to the Reds, had the same record but won the division by tiebreaker, having the better conference record. The Steelers entered the divisional round having to travel to Oakland to play the Raiders. Again. This time there was nothing immaculate about the game. God did not intervene. While a mere three-point deficit at halftime seemed promising, the Raiders completely dominated the Steelers 23-7 in the second half en route to a 33-14 thrashing of the Black and Gold. Three days before Christmas, like all of my teams in 1973, the Steelers left coal in my stocking.

The best expression of the emotion I felt after the Raiders game and as the 1973 sports year went down the toilet is contained in Don McLean's 1971 classic, "American Pie":
"And as the flames climbed high into the night
To light the sacrificial rite
I saw Satan laughing with delight
The day the music died"

The devil from Oakland, Mephistopheles in silver and black, had indeed gotten his revenge.

All in all, given the wild card designation and losing to the Raiders, it was evident that the Steelers simply weren't ready to go to the next level. Losing to Miami, the eventual Super Bowl champs, during the regular season was an omen that the Black and Gold was not ready to ascend the top of the NFL. As I mentioned earlier, strategic draft picks that began the transition from perennial losers to annual playoff contenders, while bearing fruit, did not amount to the perfect storm necessary to bring Pittsburgh a championship. However, the 1974 draft changed all of that and brought the relevant pieces together to enable the Steelers to dominate the remainder of the decade. As an illustration, the historic 1974 Pittsburgh draft went as follows (HOF indicates future Hall of Famer):

Round 1—Lynn Swann, wide receiver, USC (HOF)

Round 2—Jack Lambert, linebacker, Kent State (HOF)

Round 3—no pick

Round 4—John Stallworth, wide receiver, Alabama A&M (HOF)

Round 5—Mike Webster, center, Wisconsin (HOF)

Rounding out the group was South Carolina State's Donnie Shell, who went undrafted but was also signed by the Steelers in 1974. Shell, nicknamed the "Human Torpedo" spent the next fourteen years firing his body at opposing running backs, slamming into receivers' sides, hawking fifty-one interceptions from beguiled quarterbacks, and propelling himself straight into Canton, Ohio.

Add this group to the other future Hall of Famers already on the team—Harris, Greene, Bradshaw, Ham, and Blount, as well as perennial All-Pros and Pro Bowlers, Greenwood, White, Russell, Wagner, Edwards, and company—and the Steelers had put together a team that boasted the toughest defense in the league, a dependable one-thousand-yard rusher in Franco Harris and the potential for a first-rate passing attack.

The additions of Swann and Stallworth would give the Steelers the skill and speed on the outside to compete with the Cliff Branches, Fred Biletnikoffs, and Paul Warfields of the AFC and the Drew Pearsons and John Gilliams of the NFC. Adding Lambert to the middle linebacker position, as the axis point in the already developed Steel Curtain, made a mean, nasty, and tough defense even meaner, nastier, and tougher.

As 1974 got underway and the first half of the season progressed, the last place I thought the Steelers would end up would be in the Super Bowl. On July 1, 1974, the NFL Players Association went on strike over a dispute with the league regarding free agency, an issue, as it turned out, would take another twenty years to resolve. The players ended the walkout on August 10, opting to get back to work and deciding to let the courts hash out the grievance over time.

The effect on the Steelers, which is all that mattered to me, was that Terry Bradshaw had missed a portion of the preseason, and Head Coach Chuck Noll, who had a tumultuous relationship with Bradshaw, declared that the quarterback position was open to competition.

The result led to the opening day quarterback against the Baltimore Colts, instead of going under center wearing number twelve, wore a black and gold jersey that bore the number seventeen. And, by the way, he was Black.

Joe Gilliam, nicknamed "Jefferson Street Joe," from the Nashville neighborhood where he grew up, had outperformed both Terry Hanratty and Bradshaw in the preseason and won the starting job. Joe Willie Gillie, Gilliam's other nickname, was a takeoff on Joe "Willie" Namath and was bestowed on him from the combination of his powerful throwing arm and the white cleats he wore. A graduate of Tennessee State, Gilliam had been drafted in the eleventh round of the 1972 draft. Coming into the '74 season, Gilliam, like Hanratty, had previously been given only limited playing time.

As he took on the starting role, Gilliam would have to face two demons, one external and one internal.

Externally, he had to deal with western Pennsylvania racists. Despite an impressive 4-1-1 start, Gilliam was confronted with racial slurs and threats of violence and even death. Along with the stress of being the first Black quarterback to start in the postmerger NFL on opening day, the pressure from racial intimidation must have been enormous.

It didn't surprise me that, despite the number of beloved African American Steelers players that had captured the heart of the city, racial animus existed in western Pennsylvania. First, at the time, it was one thing to worship a defensive line that terrorized opposing quarterbacks and was made up of Black players. It was easy to adore a running back that slashed through opposing teams' defenses and who had ignited the dreams of a playoff victory with the greatest play in football history. Besides, his mother was Italian. Franco was paesano. A Black quarterback, starting on opening day, I assume for some Pittsburgh fans, was a different matter.

I have no problem believing that some, if not many, western Pennsylvania residents were, to put it mildly, not prepared to welcome a Black quarterback to Three Rivers. On a number of occasions, I remember hearing our neighbor, or someone else, perhaps at one of those softball games, referring to African Americans as "boogies." This reprehensible term was one that my parents made clear to me should be ignored and *never* repeated.

This edict was instilled in me at an early age. I can remember a dinner table conversation when I was very young, no more than first or second grade, where I recounted a story from school and repeated something that was said by a classmate at the time. I couldn't tell you the substance of the student's anecdote, but in trying to quote the lad, I barely got as far as pronouncing part of the word, "ni—." Stopped midsentence by my parents, I was scolded in a way that parents speak when parents really mean business. This was a much stronger tone than the typical, "leave your sisters alone and stop fighting," directives. This pronouncement was made, unequivocally, that such a word was inappropriate and would not be tolerated in our house, ever!

I believe my parents developed their attitudes toward race and prejudice as my father grew up in neighborhoods where many of his schoolmates and friends were Jews. My mother, I assumed, had come from such an impoverished upbringing that she didn't feel she had the luxury of feeling as if she was better than anyone. I also recall a story that my Aunt Marie would tell of a Black woman who had once saved my mother from choking by sticking her hand down her throat and dislodging a coin she had swallowed, the 1930s precursor to the Heimlich maneuver, perhaps. Plus, in the end, both my parents were just good people.

Alternatively, the internal demon Gilliam fought was drugs. Cocaine and heroin to be exact. By Gilliam's own admission, he first used drugs early on, after a week-three 17-0 drubbing by the Raiders. There were signs too. Late arrivals to practice and missed team meetings became more and more frequent. Also, as Michael MacCambridge points out in his biography of Chuck Noll, it was the Black players that saw Gilliam out at bars and clubs on occasion either using or trying to score drugs. Although drugs destroyed Gilliam's life down the road, it is hard to believe it was the *sole*, or even the major reason for his being benched two weeks after the Raiders game and despite having led the team to two additional wins.

In my opinion, however, Chuck Noll and the Rooneys would not likely let race sway their decision to bench Gilliam. I find it hard to believe that the organization that started Gilliam in the first place and who would later push for the Rooney Rule, requiring interviews for new NFL head coaches to include minority candidates, would bend to the pressure of Pittsburgh-area racists. More likely, they were appalled by it, and it emboldened them to play Gilliam.

Above all, I always believed it was simply Noll's football philosophy that led to the decision to bench Gilliam. Noll's game was defense, the running game, and ball control. Gilliam's game was passing. A lot. In his five starts, he threw the ball 198 times for 91 completions, just over 1,200 yards, four touchdowns against eight interceptions. Against Denver, a 35-35 tie, Gilliam put the ball up fifty times, unheard of for a Steelers quarterback at the time. As a starter, Gilliam only ran the ball

14 times for 41 yards. In contrast, Bradshaw, in one more start that season, threw only 146 times for a ball-controlled 776 yards, seven touchdowns, and seven interceptions. The bigger Bradshaw, 6 feet 3 inches, 215 pounds, ran the ball 34 times for 224 yards (Gilliam was 6 feet 2 inches, 187 pounds).

Bradshaw, despite his own sparring with the head coach during his career, fit Noll's vision of what a quarterback should be. This would be a stubborn philosophy that hurt the organization as the seventies turned into the eighties. In 1983, with homegrown Dan Marino available in the draft and Bradshaw and the rest of the Steel Curtain dynasty reaching the end of their careers, Noll chose a nose tackle, Gabe Rivera, over Marino. Sticking with his 1970s recipe, Noll was content to stress big defense, a strong running game, and opting for big lugs like Cliff Stoudt and Mark Malone to conservatively steer the offensive ship. Meanwhile, teams like the 49ers with their West Coast offense and the high-flying Dolphins led by Marino had changed the way NFL offenses played. Sadly, Jefferson Street Joe may have been ahead of his time, as his style could have flourished in the pass-centric 1980s.

Controversy and turmoil aside, the Steelers managed to stay focused on the field, particularly the defense, and finished with a 10-3-1 record and easily won the AFC Central. After dispatching with O. J. Simpson and the Buffalo Bills 32-14 in the divisional round, the Steelers would once again have to square off against the Raiders.

The playoff tennis match between the Steelers and the Raiders, that is, a tennis match played with clubs instead of racquets, resurfaced in 1974 as the two squads met in the first of what would be three straight AFC championship matchups.

The Steelers had the third-best record among the division winners that year at 10-3-1. The Raiders had the best record in the conference at 12-2 and, once they beat Miami in the divisional round, would host the championship game in Oakland. Raiders head coach John Madden, forever kvetching about the Immaculate Reception game, proclaimed after the hard-fought win over the Dolphins, "[W]hen the best plays the best, anything can happen." Other players, analysts, and pundits had also characterized the Raiders-Dolphins game as Super Bowl VIII ½. *Sports Illustrated*, in the December 23, 1974, issue, ran a story, penned by the legendary sportswriter Dan Jenkins that claimed the Miami-Oakland divisional playoff game was "the real Super Bowl…"

Noll and the Steelers took umbrage to this taunt and proceeded to wear the provocation as not a chip but a cinder block on their shoulders. The Black and Gold would then take that cinder block off of their shoulders and beat the Raiders senseless with it on their home turf in the championship game, 24-13, scoring twenty-one points to Oakland's three in the fourth quarter.

The stage was now set for the Steelers to win the franchise's first championship. A feat the fans had been yearning for forty years and more recently, since fucking Larry Seiple and the Dolphins had dashed their hopes two years earlier.

The Steelers' opponents vying with them for the Lombardi Trophy were the Minnesota Vikings, a team that already appeared in the big game twice, losing Super Bowl III to the Kansas City Chiefs and the prior year to the Dolphins in Super Bowl VIII.

As mentioned, defense and the running game dominated football in the 1970s, and these two teams playing in Super Bowl IX were experts at it. They both made their living this way. Like the Steel Curtain, the Vikings were no slouches on defense and had their own formidable unit on that side of the ball. The "Purple People Eaters" boasted their own cadre of future Hall of Famers that menaced opposing offenses during the Forgettable Decade. Carl Eller, Alan Page, and Jim Marshall led this band of violet-clad corsairs, channeling the Norse plunderers of yore that had sacked the coasts of medieval Britain, Scotland, and Ireland.

And while defensive tackle Doug Sutherland had the only name on the back of his jersey of Scandinavian origin, the Vikings did have their fair share of Teutonic surnames. Wally Hilgenberg, Paul Krause, and Jeff Siemon rounded out Minnesota's Purple People Eaters.

The offense was led by the wily and slippery Fran Tarkington at quarterback who had started his career in Minnesota but was exiled to the New York Giants in the late 1960s and early 1970s. Luckily for Minnesota fans, in 1972 the heady Giants traded Tarkington back to the Land of 1,000 Lakes in exchange for wide receiver Bob Grim, a dependable pass catcher on a group of otherwise pathetic Giants teams; quarterback Norm Snead, who in two and a half years with the Giants threw for 4,405 yards, twenty-seven touchdowns, and forty-one interceptions; and some players to be named later that remained nameless. Actually, one of those players, Brad Van Pelt, turned out to be a solid linebacker, anchoring the defense on another group of subsequent, otherwise pathetic Giants teams.

The Vikings also had an explosive second-year running back in Chuck Foreman who could slice through a defense on both running and passing plays and a talented wide receiver in John Gilliam who was adept at getting behind even the best of opposing secondaries. Finally, the Vikings ran the ball behind a massive offensive line led by a center with another Germanic surname, Mick Tingelhoff.

Super Bowl IX was played on January 12, 1975, at Tulane Stadium in New Orleans. It was the second-coldest Super Bowl on record, surpassed only by Super Bowl V, also played at Tulane Stadium. After these two chilly contests, the Super Bowl would not return to New Orleans until 1978, after the construction of the Louisiana Superdome.

The temperature at kickoff was forty-six degrees. The low reached forty-two. The weather was damp. It was overcast, and the winds howled at fifteen to twenty miles per hour, making for chillier conditions than what the mercury was reading. Wind gusts were over twenty-five miles per hour at times, a situation that would wreak havoc with the kickers all day.

I suspect for most fans, Super Bowl IX would be characterized as mundane, a bore, a snoozer. A type of game where having a teaser bet on the game, being in a Super Bowl pool, and consuming large amounts of alcohol and food were necessary for viewers to get through the evening.

For me, however, and I assume Steelers and Vikings fans, the game was a heart-pounding, gut-wrenching, nail-biting affair, dominated by defense, kicking miscues, and the dropsies.

The entire first half was excruciating. A summary of both teams' first-half possessions went as follows:

Pittsburgh, 3 and out;

Minnesota, 4 and out;

Pittsburgh, 5 and out;

Minnesota, 3 and out;

Pittsburgh, 6 plays, missed field goal;

Minnesota, 3 and out;

Pittsburgh, 7 plays, missed field goal on fumbled snap;

Minnesota, 5 and out;

Pittsburgh, 4 plays, fumble recovered by Minnesota at Pittsburgh 24;

Minnesota, 3 plays, missed field goal;

Pittsburgh, 6 plays and out;

Minnesota, 2 plays, Tarkington tackled in end zone, safety;

Pittsburgh, 3 and out;

Minnesota, 10 plays, Tarkington intercepted at Pittsburgh 5;

Pittsburgh, 4 plays, end of half.

Halftime score: Pittsburgh 2, Minnesota 0.

Super Bowl IX was an ugly game. Ugly from the standpoint of chilly temperatures, swirling winds, and seven total turnovers. Five by Minnesota. The Steelers were penalized 122 yards on 8 infractions. The teams' respective placekickers missed three field goals and an extra point, and a blocked punt led to the Vikings' only score.

However, it was the type of ugly I had gotten used to as a Steelers fan. In many ways, it is the type of game I would have to deal with every season, year after year, for the next half century. And I loved it. The games epitomized what Pittsburgh football was all about, heart palpitations aside.

The Steel Curtain was so dominant that day that they held the Vikings to seventeen yards rushing on twenty-one attempts, a staggering twenty-nine inches per carry. The defense picked off Tarkington three times and took away two fumbles. The Steelers smothered the Vikings in every phase of the game.

On the other side of the ball, Pittsburgh amassed 333 yards of total offense compared to Minnesota's 119, including a Super Bowl record 158 rushing yards for Franco Harris, a record that would stand until the Redskins' John Riggins's 1983 trampling over the Miami Dolphins, whose defense, by the way, was no Purple People Eaters. Harris's mark is still fourth all-time, and Franco's 354 total yards in four Super Bowls still tops all players in NFL history.

◆◆◆

Now, with a championship under their belts, the 1975 season brought additional anticipation for the Steelers. The draft picks from 1969–1973 had matured. The 1974 selections from the college ranks were another year older and were melding with the team on both offense and defense. The quarterback controversy was over.

Pittsburgh finished the regular season with the best record in the AFC and tied for the league's best at 12-2. After dispatching with the Baltimore Colts in the divisional round, it was time once again for a classic Steelers-Raiders matchup, this time the game was to be played at a frigid Three Rivers Stadium. With temperatures in the teens and the windchill further dropping the mercury to just above zero, the game would be played on a frozen artificial turf field. Two things, of course, happened. One, it was another hard-fought, close game, and, two, the Raiders whined about the field conditions, claiming it hampered their ability to execute their offense. As was usually the case, all of the boo-hooing from the Raiders fails to consider the fact that, Pittsburgh, too, had to play in the same conditions. As for hard fought, the score was three to zero, Steelers, at the end of the third quarter. Both teams combined for twelve turnovers, the Steelers committing seven of them.

Of course, it wouldn't have been a Steelers game if the Black and Gold didn't try and make it interesting. In the fourth quarter, with the Raiders down 16-7 and, therefore, needing two scores to win and time running out, the Silver and Black opted for a forty-one-yard field goal with only twelve seconds left. For some reason, the Steelers must have felt that they had to keep their fans interested as Oakland recovered the ensuing onside kick, giving them one more shot at victory. Ken Stabler launched a forty-yard bomb that was reeled in by wide receiver Cliff Branch at the Pittsburgh fifteen. Branch, however, was tackled inbounds and time expired. Final score: Steelers 16, Raiders 10.

In the end, for the second year in a row, the Steelers had beaten the hated Raiders in the championship game. They, once again, earned the right to play for the NFL championship to try and accomplish what only Lombardi's Packers and Shula's Dolphins had done, win consecutive Super Bowls.

As it turned out, Super Bowl X would pit my Pittsburgh Steelers against the Dallas Cowboys, a team as equally despised by me as the Raiders. However, my animus for the Cowboys was of a different nature. I had no dog in the fight in the NFC and, therefore, didn't really care who won or lost. But the Cowboys always seemed to win, always seemed to get the breaks, and always seemed to have the referees on their side. They were the 1970s version of Belichick and Brady's Patriots.

Dallas Coach Tom Landry was touted as the "genius" of his time and was an offensive innovator. Although he did not invent the shotgun formation, he was the first to implement it on a regular basis into his offense. Additionally, the Cowboys did this annoying presnap cadence on offense. When they came up to the line of scrimmage and were preparing to get set for the snap of the ball, quarterback Roger Staubach would call, "Shift!" or, "Let's do good!" or, "Let's be assholes," or something to that effect. The Dallas offense would then stand upright before returning to their three-point stances. This annoyed the shit out of me.

I further detested them because, whenever possible, they were among only a few teams, including the loathsome Dolphins, who insisted on wearing their white uniforms at home. As most teams wore dark jerseys at home, the Cowboys also got to wear white on the road. As I said, the Cowboys always seemed to get their way.

Now these criticisms may seem a bit petty, but for the passionate sports fan these emotions are the essence of the love-hate relationship. This insistence on wearing white was just another reason for hating Dallas.

Super Bowl X, like the previous year, would also feature dominant defensive performances, kicking foibles, and heart palpitations, yet, unlike the previous year, the game would be perceived as anything but boring.

On a late, sunny, January 18th afternoon in Miami at the Orange Bowl, Dallas won the toss and elected to receive. Upon corralling the kickoff, Preston Pearson, who had played for the Steelers in 1974 and received a Super Bowl ring, handed the ball off on a reverse to Dallas's brash and cocky rookie and resident dickhead, Thomas "Hollywood" Henderson. The move caught the Steelers off guard, and Henderson returned the ball forty-eight yards to the Pittsburgh forty-four. He might have gone all the way had it not been for Roy Gerela's heroics. Gerela, the last man standing between Henderson and the end zone, threw his body at Henderson, knocking him down and out of bounds. But the touchdown-saving tackle proved costly as Gerela badly bruised his ribs on the play, leaving him with nagging pain throughout the game and, as we'll see, greatly impacted his ability to kick.

At the time, there were no Erin Andrews, Pam Olivers, or Tracy Wolfsons patrolling the sideline for up-to-the-minute injury reports. CBS announcers Pat Summerall and Tom Brookshire would comment on Gerela's kicking mishaps throughout the afternoon, never mentioning the injury.

After Tom Landry's kickoff shenanigans and despite the good field position that it yielded, the Steelers, probably pissed, held the Cowboys to a three and out that garnered a net minus three yards. Pittsburgh's first possession went only slightly better, gaining one first down before failing to convert on a third and one and having to give the ball back to the Cowboys. But punter Bobby Walden muffed the snap, and Dallas recovered the miscue, giving them new life and great field position at the Steelers' twenty-nine yard line.

One play after the Walden snafu, Staubach hit Drew Pearson on a crossing route, and the Dallas wide receiver outran the Steelers' secondary into the end zone. Stunningly, just like that, it was Dallas 7, Steelers 0.

The Steelers wasted no time, however, in getting even. Eight plays and sixty-seven yards after the kickoff, highlighted by a thirty-two-yard acrobatic sideline grab by Lynn Swann and capped off by a seven-yard pass to tight end Randy Grossman, the Steelers were even. Swann would make two such catches that afternoon, exhibiting footwork and concentration that would've made Mikhail Baryshnikov jealous. Steelers 7, Cowboys 7.

On their next possession, Dallas drove downfield, only to have the drive stall at the Pittsburgh nineteen. As the first quarter spilled into the beginning of the second, Dallas's healthy-ribbed kicker, Tony Fritsch, put the Cowboys back on top, 10-7.

The two squads would spar without incident for the majority of the second quarter, until, aided by another amazing catch by Swann, this one better than the last, the Steelers advanced the ball down to the Dallas nineteen. With the clock winding down, and, from the identical distance as Fritsch, thirty-six yards (the goalposts are now at the back of the end zone), the battered and bruised Gerela hooked the kick, wide left. Dallas went into the halftime break leading 10-7. Despite the three-point deficit, it bears noting that that vaunted Steelers defense, although quietly, was beginning to take control of the game.

The Fritsch field goal occurred ten seconds into the second quarter. For the balance of the quarter, fourteen minutes and fifty seconds, and with the Steelers failing to score themselves, when the halftime gun sounded, America's Team compiled a total of only twenty-one net yards of offense.

Things did not get much better for Dallas in the second half. On their first possession of the third quarter, the Cowboys had only progressed three yards when cornerback J. T. Thomas picked off Staubach's third-down pass for the first of three Steelers interceptions. Thomas returned the ball thirty-five yards to the Dallas twenty-five, giving the Steelers excellent field position.

To the average fan or an outside observer, it may be difficult to appreciate the level of dominance exhibited by the Steelers' defense, especially since the Cowboys held the lead from the beginning of the second quarter until around twelve minutes left in the game. Following the Thomas pick, however, the Cowboy D dug in, forcing another field goal attempt. Once again, Gerela hooked the kick, this time from thirty-three yards.

After the miss, the usually disciplined and businesslike Cowboys went off script, or, more accurately, royally screwed up. Apparently, number forty-three, safety Cliff Harris, just couldn't resist the temptation to taunt Gerela after his botched attempt, patting him on his helmet as if to say, "Thanks for missing…again." Unbeknownst to Harris, standing only a few yards away was Jack Lambert, who rushed to his teammate's aid, grabbed Harris, and tossed the white *jersied* schmuck to the ground. The play got the Steelers revved up, in other words pissed off, and the game would change definitively from that point on. The Steel Curtain's dominance over the Dallas offensive attack would no longer be quiet.

After Lambert's public spanking of the Dallas free safety and with about ten minutes left in the third, the Cowboys were forced to punt after running five plays and gaining twenty yards. A more productive drive ensued on their next possession, but a senseless clipping penalty by running back Robert Newhouse after only a two-yard Staubach scramble followed by more Steel Curtain tenacity led to another punt, capping an eight-play drive that yielded only twenty-nine yards.

All along, however, during this stretch, as the Steel Curtain was battering Tom Landry's squad, the Steelers offense remained fairly anemic and was not capitalizing on all of the opportunities the defense was providing. But things were about to change.

On their first possession of the fourth quarter, the Cowboys amassed, bookended by sacks from defensive tackle Steve Furness and defensive end L. C. Greenwood, a net minus three yards. The three-play mugging of the Dallas offense forced the Cowboys to boot the ball back to the Steelers with punter Mitch Hoopes's heels resting in the goal line.

On the snap, special teams player Reggie Harrison tore through the middle of the formation and blocked Hoopes's punt, slapping the ball out of the end zone and giving the Black and Gold a two-point safety. Dallas 10, Steelers 9.

The punt block and safety came at 11:56 of the fourth quarter. For the next eight minutes and twenty-five seconds, the previously somnambulistic Steelers offense finally decided to join the defense and unleashed a force on both sides of the ball that rivaled a Spring tornado touching down and ripping through Big D.

During that time frame, it was all Steelers. Following the free kick after the safety, the Steelers drove twenty-five yards in six plays. This time neither Gerela's foot nor aching ribs failed him, and he connected from thirty-six yards. Steelers 12, Cowboys 10.

On the first play of Dallas's next possession, safety Mike Wagner stepped in front of Staubach's pass intended for Drew Pearson and returned it nineteen yards to the Dallas seven. Doomsday stiffened again, however, and for the second time in about two minutes, Gerela was called on once more to put the ball through the uprights. The leader of the Gorillas kick was true again, this time from eighteen yards. Steelers 15, Dallas 10.

The Cowboys went three and out on their next possession, aided by another L. C. Greenwood sack, the Curtain's sixth of the game. Taking possession on their own thirty after another Hoopes punt, Bradshaw and company faced a third and four. Initially having time to throw, but with the pocket breaking down, Bradshaw stood in and launched a sixty-plus-yard missile at a streaking Lynn Swann on a post pattern. Swann beat Cowboy defensive back Mark Washington like a drum, gathered in the pass at the six and galloped into the end zone. With just over three minutes left on the clock, Gerela missed his third kick of the day, hooking the extra point. Steelers 21, Cowboys 10.

The touchdown seemingly put the game out of reach, that is, except for two factors. First, upon releasing the ball, the exposed Bradshaw was cheap-shotted with a helmet-to-helmet hit, a clear violation under today's Article 11, from Dallas defensive tackle and cement-headed douchebag Larry Cole. The vicious hit laid out the Pittsburgh signal caller who had to be helped off the field. Bradshaw would be out for the rest of the game, having suffered a concussion.

The second reason? They were still playing Roger Staubach and the Cowboys. Three weeks earlier in the divisional playoff game in Minnesota, Staubach hit wide receiver Drew Pearson on a fifty-yard bomb with thirty-two seconds left and snatched almost certain victory from the Vikings. The "Hail Mary" pass play was controversial as many, including one of my best friends, Willie, who was a rabid Vikings fan, thought that Pearson had pushed off Vikings cornerback Nate Wright in order to haul in the pass. Now, with three minutes left on the clock and Bradshaw in the locker room, some form of possible repeat performance was weighing heavy on the minds of Steelers fans, including me.

But with the Black and Gold having such a comfortable lead, what could really go wrong? As Steelers' faithful have learned over the years, all that could go wrong was *everything*. And it almost did.

After a Gerela touchback, Staubach took over on his own twenty, again, with just under three minutes to go. Taking advantage of the Steelers' "prevent defense," a tactic that any old man at the end of the bar will tell you only prevents victory, the Cowboys drove to the Pittsburgh thirty-four-yard line in four plays. With 1:56 on the clock, Mel Blount tripped while covering wide receiver Percy Howard who took a pass from Staubach falling backward in the end zone. Steelers 21, Cowboys 17.

With an onside kick looming, the only thing the Steelers had to do was fall on the ball, get one first down, and run out the clock in order to cement their victory. The first of these tasks was accomplished with precision as offensive lineman Gerry Mullins fell on the ball. However, acts two and three of this end-of-game drama would have to play themselves out without Bradshaw behind center and with Terry Hanratty at the helm.

With Dallas using their three timeouts after each play, the Steelers gained a total of one yard on three running plays. Hanratty, much like his appearance in the 1972 championship game, had little playing time in

1975, and with the "don't fuck things up" backup quarterback rule clearly in effect, the Steelers dove straight ahead on a trio of runs.

Next, astonishing the crowd, the announcers, and me, instead of punting on fourth down, Chuck Noll opted to run the ball one more time. Rocky Bleier did so for two yards, and the Steelers turned the ball over on downs with 1:22 on the clock, handing the ball back to the Cowboys at the Dallas thirty-nine-yard line.

At first blush, Noll's decision appears to fall somewhere between inexplicable and downright idiotic. The gamble, however, was explained by the Pittsburgh skipper after the game. Apparently, Noll was wary about the Steelers' punting situation. Veteran Bobby Walden had fumbled the team's first punt, and, although he recovered it, the good field position set Dallas up for its first score of the game. The Cowboys had also come close on a couple of other occasions to blocking Walden's kicks. Therefore, Noll opted to try for the first down, rather than risk disaster. If unsuccessful, he would rely on his Steel Curtain, the squad that had gotten them there, to shut down the Cowboys.

Now, with no timeouts and the prevent defense back on the field, Staubach went to work again. On first down, Staubach, harassed by only a Steelers front three, scrambled for eleven yards to midfield. Next, a pass to Preston Pearson for twelve yards to the Steelers' thirty-eight. But with no ability to stop the clock, Staubach was reduced to going for the end zone in an effort to create a miracle ending. As he did against the Vikings, Roger the Dodger threw up a Hail Mary. The pass fell incomplete. He then tried an Our Father. Again, the pass was knocked away. Finally, Staubach hoisted up an Act of Contrition, but, on this Sunday, his prayers were not answered, and the last of the three passes was tipped by Wagner and corralled in by safety Glen Edwards who ran up the field as time expired, allowing my blood pressure to return to normal systolic and diastolic levels and sealing the Steelers' victory.

On that celebrated Sunday, the good guys, wearing black, beat the bad guys, who wore white. Pittsburgh won their second Super Bowl in a row. In four short years, the franchise had gone from laughing stocks to legends.

Chapter 10
Here Come the Yankees

The season after the Murcer trade to San Francisco was fallow, at least in terms of Yankees baseball success. About three months after Bobby Murcer was dispatched to the West Coast, the Steelers won their first Super Bowl ring. However, the euphoria from gridiron accomplishments did not duplicate themselves on the baseball diamond. The Pirates fell short in the 1974 NLCS three games to one to the Dodgers and would soon lose their grip on the National League East, taking a three-year hiatus in favor of their cross-state rivals, the Phillies. The Yankees' indentured servitude at Shea would continue for another year, through the 1975 season. That year, the Yanks finished in third place, twelve games behind Boston.

It was a different time in terms of where my love-hate compass pointed as it related to the Red Sox since Boston had been more or less irrelevant as an adversary since I began following baseball in earnest. The Orioles, not the Red Sox, were the Yankees' hated rival.

In fact, except for the Pirates, I either didn't give a shit about, hated, or fucking hated the entire National League. Therefore, in every fall classic I pulled for the American League. This included, as I alluded to earlier, rooting for the Sox in the 1975 Series against the Reds. Once again, for the third time in six years, Cincinnati had ousted the Pirates from the playoffs, this time by outscoring the Bucs nineteen to seven in an embarrassing three-game sweep in the NLCS. In 1975, I hated the fucking Reds. I didn't give a shit about the Red Sox.

Of course, this would all change a year later in 1976 when one of the all-time great Red Sox players and cry babies, Carlton Fisk, took issue with a play at the plate involving Lou Pinella. A bench-emptying brawl ensued, and Boston, without passing go, moved directly into the "fucking hate" category.

The Murcer-for-Bonds trade, traumatic as it was, began, in an unexpected way, to bear fruit on December 11, 1975, when George Steinbrenner set out to make good on his promise to bring championships and glory back to the Bronx. With the 1975 NFL playoffs not yet underway and the Steelers' road to becoming a dynastic Super Bowl powerhouse still an open question, the Yankees front office began to make some moves.

After only one season, Bobby Bonds had apparently overstayed his welcome with the Bombers and was traded to the California Angels for pitcher Ed Figueroa and center fielder Mickey, "Mick the Quick," Rivers.

Also, on that December day, the Yankees traded starter Doc Medich, who had gone 49-40 in his three-year tenure in pinstripes to the Pirates for Ken Brett, Dock Ellis, and Willie Randolph. The journeyman Brett had done yeoman's work for the Pirates, going 22-14, but would have only a cup of coffee in New York, being almost immediately dispatched to the Chicago White Sox in May for Carlos May, who would be a piece, albeit a small piece, of the puzzle that got the Yanks to the World Series in 1976 and 1977. Ellis, who had always been a bit of a head case, even by Pirates standards, had been a contributor to the early 70s Pirates successes, including throwing a no-hitter in 1970, and was part of the 1971 World Series championship team. Ellis would disappear from the

Yankees' roster in the first month of the 1977 season, but his 17-8 record was a major contribution to New York's appearance in the 1976 World Series after emerging from their twelve-year pennant slumber.

Randolph, however, was the diamond in the rough. He would become one of the foundations of the late '70s Yankees dynasty and go on to be named Yankees captain in 1986, one of the successors to Thurman Munson after Munson's tragic 1979 death.

Even prior to this late 1975 flurry of activity, Steinbrenner had already made some moves to try and put the championship pieces into place. About a year before, he signed Oakland A's ace and 1974 Cy Young winner, Catfish Hunter, as a free agent, baseball's first, to a multiyear, multimillion-dollar contract. The season prior, the Yanks acquired "Sweet Lou" Piniella from the Kansas City Royals. And in three different years, the front office picked the pocket of the Cleveland Indians acquiring Graig Nettles in 1972, Chris Chambliss in 1974, and Oscar Gamble in 1975.

All of these players would be favorites of mine and were all major contributors to the team's first playoff appearance since 1964. In 1976, the trio of Hunter, Figueroa, and Ellis combined for a total of fifty-three wins against only thirty-five losses. With the exception of Gamble, who would return in 1980, and Ellis, all of these players stayed through the balance of the decade and were part of the 1977 and 1978 championship teams.

Also, in August of 1975, Steinbrenner fired manager Bill Virdon, who barely had the team over .500 at 53-51. The Virdon firing would be the first in a multidecades-long ritual that amounted to, on average, a manager change every year and a half. In his place, he brought in former Yankee Billy Martin, who, as a manager, had a reputation of turning bad teams around and making them contenders. "Billyball" worked its magic three times during Martin's tenures with the Minnesota Twins, Detroit Tigers, and Texas Rangers. However, Martin had another reputation too, namely, being a hot head who, to put it mildly, enjoyed imbibing in the demon rum. Despite being a fan favorite, sooner or later, Martin's mouth, his drinking, or his temper—sometimes all three in concert—wore out his welcome despite the success he had turning around the franchises he coached.

During his playing days in the Bronx, Billy also had been a favorite of legendary manager Casey Stengel and played on four World Series teams in the 1950s, earning a reputation as a clutch, gritty, scrapper of a player. He was also a member of the Yankee Rat Pack, along with Whitey Ford, Mickey Mantle, Yogi Berra, and Hank Bauer, notorious for their off-the-field and after-hours antics, which included a late-night brawl at Manhattan's famed Copacabana Nightclub in 1957. The incident led to Martin being traded the following day to Kansas City.

Temper and reputation aside, for purposes of Steinbrenner's transformation project, Billy had the perfect pedigree to take the Yankee helm.

In any event, the seeds planted back in the Murcer trade now took root, and Steinbrenner's maneuvering, along with Martin's arrival, brought great anticipation that 1976 would be a special year. In fact, the Yankees got out to a strong start that year and never looked back.

By June 1, the Yanks were five games in front of the second-place Orioles. At the All-Star break, they were nine and a half games ahead of the Red Sox. On September 15, the Bombers extended their lead to ten and a half games, again, over Baltimore—the same position where they would be at season's end.

Resurrected, the Yankees' opponents for their first shot at a pennant in a dozen years were the Kansas City Royals. In 1976, the Royals had beaten out the free-agent-riddled Oakland A's who had won the AL West every year since 1971. Kansas City combined a formidable offense with a relatively no-name, but highly effective pitching staff that notched ninety wins during the season to finish ahead of the Athletics by two and a half games. Led by AL batting champ George Brett, smooth fielding, solid hitting center fielder Amos Otis, and sluggers John Mayberry and Hal McRae at first base and DH, respectively, the Royals had taken the season series against the Yankees in 1976, winning seven of the twelve games played that year. While the Yanks and their fans beamed with confidence, this was, by no means, going to be a piece of cake. I hated the royal blue–clad team from Kansas City. Brett, with his tobacco-stuffed cheek drew my particular ire, as he always seemed to have the Yankees' number when he stepped into the batter's box.

Ann's Bakery and the Promised Land

The tight contest that was the 1976 ALCS began on October 9, 1976, in Kansas City. In what would turn out to be an evenly matched series right up until the last pitch of the last inning of the last game, the two teams went right to form and split games one and two.

Returning to the Bronx, the Yanks and Dock Ellis, despite giving up three runs in the first inning, won game three. With the pennant within their grasp, Billy Martin gambled and pitched Catfish Hunter in game four on only three days' rest. The decision backfired as Hunter couldn't get through the fourth inning, gave up five runs, and took the loss. The stage was now set for a dramatic game five at the stadium.

As best as I can recall, most of Thursday, October 14, 1976, was an unremarkable day; however, by early evening the day took a momentous turn. Surprising the family that afternoon, my father came home early, much earlier than expected. *The Old Farmer's Almanac* for 1976 says that sunset on October 14 of that year occurred at 6:15 p.m., confirming my memory that my father had arrived early as it was a mid-October afternoon and there was still plenty of light out.

As previously mentioned, my father worked for the Great Atlantic & Pacific Tea Company, a.k.a. the A&P. Pulling into our driveway on Candlewood Drive, he got out of his red A&P refrigeration van and enthusiastically explained the reason for his premature arrival. "Get ready," he said, "Ann's Bakery gave me two tickets to tonight's game!"

Ann and Sal Lovetere owned an Italian bakery (officially, the Grassy Sprain Bakery) on Tuckahoe Road in a strip center that was our one-stop for after-church Sunday shopping during the Forgettable Decade. The shopping center also boasted a candy store (Max's), a Chinese take-out place (Ping Pong) owned by the parents of our high school's valedictorian and his sister, Billy and Susan Low. There was an Italian restaurant with a bar that anchored the right side of the plaza, DeFemio's, featuring live music with the owner, Al DeFemio, on drums. It was also rumored to be a watering hole for one of our schoolmate's fathers who enjoyed a drink or two or five before heading home to the family. Centering the row of stores was Toy Warehouse (officially the Toy and Sports Warehouse), the mecca for everything from Barbie dolls, Easy Bake Ovens, G.I. Joes, and Hot Wheels to helmets, shoulder pads, jockstraps, and baseball gloves—all the necessary items any boy or girl needed to make their way in a kid's world. On Sundays, and with New York State's Blue Laws in effect for much of the decade, Max's and Ann's were the only two stops that were on our itinerary.

Max's was for the kids. It was where I purchased my weekly supply of baseball cards, comic books (later wrestling magazines), and candy. Depending on my mood, it would be Sweet Tarts or a Nestlé's Crunch Bar. After Max's, I would wander over to Ann's to see how my parents' selection of bakery fare was going.

On many occasions, I would observe an odd occurrence. There would be a discussion over whether my father would either be given the rolls and Italian cookies he ordered gratis, receive them at some discounted rate, or pay for them, usually by having to leave the money on the counter and running out the door. Being a teenage boy, I never asked why these discussions were taking place. Teenage boys, with the exception of girls and sports, are oblivious to most things, so the weekly monetary tussle over baked goods went right over my head. As it turned out, my father, being a refrigeration aficionado, would do work for Ann and Sal on the side whenever a refrigerator case, condenser, or walk-in box went on the blink. Knowing my father, he probably did it for very little money, certainly well below what an outside contractor would charge. In fact, I wouldn't be surprised if, many times, he didn't charge them anything. So grateful were Ann and Sal over the years that I can remember some Christmases when we would get presents from the bakery's proprietors.

In any event, perhaps as a result of some recent repairs or, a culmination of many jobs done at the bakery, on this day my father was given tickets to the deciding game for the first chance the Yankees had at a pennant since 1964. I was ecstatic. Again being oblivious, I certainly didn't question how or why we got the tickets.

And so, on a lark and by divine intervention, we headed to the stadium. Like many games I attended in the Forgettable Decade, I do not remember chapter and verse the entire goings-on that night. There are, however, eight things I distinctly recall and that are forever etched in my memory.

1) It was cold. Actually, it was freezing, especially for the middle of October. I could consult wunderground.com again for the actual temperature, but why bother? It was cold and windy, and I was wearing a snorkel jacket. This ubiquitous parka-esque outerwear was standard attire in the mid-1970s and boasted a hood ringed with what looked like German shepherd hair.

2) The seats were really good, like great. If I had to estimate, we were about twenty rows behind the Yankees' dugout. Basically, the mirror image of the seats I had for the White Sox game that I attended with my mother a few years earlier, but a little further down the right field line. In other words, they were the Catholic heaven seats.

3) It was the first time I experienced group profanity. There were numerous chants of "KC sucks!" I believe this is important to note as it establishes Kansas City, rather than the Boston Red Sox, as original targets of the "sucks" chant.

4) There were a few game delays from fans throwing shit on the field. At times, the outfield looked like Shea Stadium did on a normal day.

5) In the top of the eighth, with a 6-3 lead and all things looking peachy, George Brett silenced 56,821 fans with a game-tying three-run homer off of Yankees reliever Grant Jackson. It was the type of silence my classmates and I might experience at Saint Eugene's while cutting up in Mr. Moody's math class and Sister Aloysia, hearing the noise from across the hall, burst through the door. Except that night, there was none of the snickering we would have done after Sister Aloysia left the classroom. In this instance, the stadium crowd was in shock.

6) With one exception, things went blank for me between the Brett home run, which came with no one out in the top of the eighth, and the bottom half of the ninth. I had to look up the who and the what of this interval for this writing. In the top of the ninth, with two out, catcher Buck Martinez singled, followed by a walk to outfielder Al Cowens. Jim Wohlford came to the plate with the go-ahead run on base. What I distinctly remember, however, was that George Brett was on deck. If, by some chance, Wohlford drew a walk, the bases would be loaded for the Yankees killer. I clearly recall hoping, no praying, that Brett would not have a chance in the batter's box again. Dick Tidrow got Wohlford to ground into a force out and that was that. I could breathe again.

7) In the bottom of the ninth, leadoff hitter Chris Chambliss faced off against the Royals' Mark Littell, who had come on in relief in the seventh and efficiently set down five Yankees in a row. After

another delay due to more garbage being thrown on the field, Chambliss took Littell's first pitch of the inning and launched it over the right-center-field wall. All hell broke loose. Fans poured onto the field. It was like Three Rivers after the Immaculate Reception, but on stronger steroids. Chambliss had to bowl people over trying to get around the bases. In a scene resembling Robert the Bruce's Scots charging the field at Bannockburn, the base paths were so obstructed that the Yankees first baseman never touched home plate and had to be escorted out after the game with a security detail to put his foot where home plate *was*. During the melee, home plate had been ripped out of the ground by the fans, and Chambliss touched the hole that was left in order to officially memorialize the home run.

8) The final thing I remember was, after the home run and the fans flooded onto the field, there was a quintessential moment of father-son nonverbal communication. I looked at my father as if to say, "Can I go out there?" He looked back with his eyes firmly replying, "Not a chance!"

The high from the dramatic win that gave the Yankees their first pennant in a dozen years carried through to the World Series that began two days later. However, that excitement was quickly extinguished. All I remember about the '76 World Series was that it was over in a blink of an eye. Chambliss's home run came late in the evening on October 14. A week later, on October 21, the Reds had swept the Yankees, won the World Series, and outscored the Bronx Bombers by a count of 22 to 8. One thing I recall was that the obnoxious Pete Rose, who I had hated ever since he plowed into Ray Fosse to end the 1970 all-star game, played up at third base in order to challenge Mickey Rivers and take the bat out of his hands. By the way, Rose should be in the Hall of Fame, but he was still a dick in my book. To add further insult to injury, the 7-2 thrashing in the game 4 embarrassment took place at the House That Ruth Built in front of over 50,000 fans.

And so, the fall continued and turned into a winter of discontent. After the World Series debacle, the Steelers made the playoffs in '76 but were beaten in the championship game by the Raiders. Just like that, it was time to wait until next year.

The Bronx Zoo

The lesson George Steinbrenner took from the absolute thrashing the Reds meted out to the Yankees in the 1976 World Series, I believe, was a similar one to what the Steelers experienced after their loss in the 1972 AFC championship game to Miami. The Yankees were good, and they had the firepower to get to the World Series, but there were still a few pieces missing in order for the Bronx Bombers to become an elite franchise and take their place among other great Yankees teams of the past.

Steinbrenner, never the patient man, got to work right away. Thirty-nine days after the four-game drubbing by the Reds, the Yankees signed free agent Reggie Jackson to a five-year contract worth around $3 million. Jackson had been a crucial part of the early '70s Oakland A's dynasty that dominated major league baseball between 1972 and 1974. Had free agency not come along and shredded the A's juggernaut, it is likely that they would have won more titles. On the other hand, if that were the case, Reggie may have never become a Yankee.

Jackson, a powerful slugger with a strong throwing arm but a mediocre glove, won the AL home run crown in 1973 and 1975 and was runner-up in '71, '74, and '76. He also garnered the RBI title in 1973, grabbing two-thirds of that year's Triple Crown. He was named World Series MVP in the A's 1973 seven-game victory of the Mets. He was outspoken and unapologetic about being so. His critics labeled him "cocky." As a Black ballplayer, Jackson's race and vociferous nature would inspire racial animus from some fans, especially when prompted by the fishbowl that was the New York media, who pitted Jackson against Manager Billy Martin.

Billy, however, didn't need any prompting from the press to have animosity against Jackson. By all measures, he didn't like Reggie, period. From my perspective, it stemmed from two factors. Race could've been a big one. Reggie certainly thought so. Second, Martin played in an era of the humble player, both Black and white. The flamboyant Jackson, who was never shy about citing his accomplishments, was anathema to Martin, who played with the "Aw Shucks" Mickey Mantle, and was a contemporary of both the serene "Say Hey" Willie Mays and the stoic Hammerin' Hank Aaron, all of which, likely in his mind, were superior players to Jackson.

Over his tenure, Jackson had run-ins with Yankees players, Munson, Mickey Rivers, and Graig Nettles, to name a few. Jackson had also alienated team members upon his arrival with the now infamous "the straw that stirs the drink" quote, which was seen as a slight of the extremely popular Yankees captain, Thurman Munson. Reggie denied the quote, but damage had been done. However, most of these fences eventually got mended. Winning world championships will do that.

For me, I was ecstatic that Reggie had landed in pinstripes, and I immediately embraced Jackson as the Yankees savior upon his arrival. After two years wandering in the baseball idol wilderness, I had found Bobby Murcer's replacement, or at least his surrogate.

In any event, as this is a book about "fond memories," I choose not to dwell on the chaos that existed over the 1977–1978 seasons. Besides, if one wants a blow-by-blow recount of the off- and sometimes on-the-field drama that took place outside of Yankees box scores, one can read, provided you can get through the tedium, Sparky Lyle's tell-all chronicle, *The Bronx Zoo*. George's seemingly daily micromanaging of the team, Billy vs. Reggie, George vs. Billy, George vs., well, everyone else.

It was irrelevant to me. What really mattered was what happened on the field, and it was, to borrow the Mets' descriptive, amazing!

There was another critical piece of the thin crust, New York–style pizza that brought championships back to the Bronx. However, this slice of the pie came from inside the organization, not free agency, and arrived without the same fanfare that Reggie did.

Ron Guidry, a.k.a. "Louisiana Lightning," a.k.a. "Gator," came up with the Yankees via the third round of the 1971 draft where, at the time, he was playing for the University of Louisiana at Lafayette. Guidry can be considered the quintessential late bloomer. Drafted at age twenty-one, he spent six years, four in the minors and two with the team, but appearing in only seventeen games over the 1975–1976 seasons. Considered trade bait over that time, to the good fortune of the Yankees, none of these transactions ever came to fruition.

Guidry appeared in earnest during the 1977 season, where he was a major contributor to that year's championship squad. Buttressing the Yankees pitching staff in a year that an injury-plagued Catfish Hunter went 9-9, Guidry finished the season 16-7 with a .282 ERA. His blazing fastball and tailing slider were a welcome complement to the balance of the starting rotation of Ed Figueroa, Mike Torrez, and Don Gullett.

In the 1977 playoff run, Guidry represented himself well, garnering two wins and a no-decision in three starts against both the Royals and the Dodgers. But this was just the tip of the iceberg.

In 1978, he posted an amazing 25-3 record with a 1.74 ERA. Guidry was dominant throughout the year. His command over opposing batters was consistent during the "Zoo" period, where he served as an anchor, keeping the team from foundering when the Yanks fell to fourteen games back. Guidry maintained this excellence through the pennant run, including nabbing the win in the one-game playoff in Boston. When the season ended and the postseason accolades were being doled out, Guidry was the hands-down choice for the American League's best pitcher. Gator

received all twenty-eight first-place votes and was overwhelmingly awarded the American League Cy Young Award. In '78, he again went 2-0 in
the playoffs and World Series.

◆◆◆

Looking back from a lens that is almost a half century old, it is sometimes
difficult to distinguish between the 1977 and 1978 championships. After
all, both years the Yankees beat Kansas City in the ALCS to win the pennant. Both October classics pitted the Yankees against the Los Angeles
Dodgers, and the Bronx Bombers took both series in six games. However,
there were some distinct contrasts.

The year 1977 was different as it was not so much of a Red Sox
collapse, as would be the case a year later, as it was a Yankees juggernaut
clicked into gear. On August 15, the Red Sox were on top of the AL East,
four and a half games ahead of New York and three and a half games
ahead of Baltimore. But the Yankees went on a tear and flipped the script
going 18-2 over the next twenty games. By September 4, they were four
and a half games ahead of the Red Sox and five games ahead of the Orioles.

From that point on, the Bronx Bombers never looked back with
neither of their main AL East rivals getting closer than one and a half
games for a day and finishing the season two and a half games ahead of
both Boston and Baltimore.

This is a major difference between baseball and the NFL, where
every week one game has major implications, especially as the postseason
draws near. In baseball, barring some sort of on-field catastrophe, it is
difficult to overcome what ostensibly appears to be a meager four-and-a-
half-game lead late in the season, even (as in the case of the '77 Yankees)
with twenty-eight games left. If the division leader merely treads water,
goes 14-14 over the span, the chasing team needs to go 19-9, a .678 win-

ning percentage, in order to surpass them. If the lead team puts together a few wins in a row down the stretch, the task to keep pace and overtake them becomes Herculean, if not impossible.

The Yankees waltzed into the playoffs and won another hard-fought ALCS battle with Kansas City, this time coming back from 2-1 down to take the last two contests. Devastating the Royals for the second year in a row, the Yanks came up in the top of the ninth in game five down 3-2. Two hits, a walk, an RBI sacrifice fly, and an error by none other than George Brett later, the Bombers won the game 5-3. Once again, the Yankees had snatched the pennant away from the Royals in dramatic fashion.

In the World Series, after splitting the first two games in New York, the Yanks won three of the next four games and dispatched the pious Los Angeleans in six. Capping off the final game was Reggie's batting clinic against the Dodger pitching staff. After a second-inning walk on four pitches, Jackson hit three home runs on three consecutive pitches, including a mammoth blast on his last at bat deep into the former center field bleachers area that had been blacked out when the stadium was re-modeled. His performance won him his second World Series MVP award of the decade and cemented his reputation as Mr. October.

The year 1978, on the other hand, was a different matter entirely.

Yes, the Yankees beat the Royals again in the ALCS, this time in four games. And despite dropping the first two games at a repeat World Series match against the Dodgers, the Yanks won four straight contests, led by an unlikely duo of heroes. While the credit for the delayed sweep of the Dodgers can be attributed to all of the Yankees, a full team effort, the headlines were grabbed rookie Brian Doyle and shortstop Bucky Dent, the number eight and nine batters in the lineup. Doyle, who was filling in for the injured Willie Randolph, batted .438 in the series, scored four runs, and batted in two more. Dent would secure World Series MVP honors, buttressed by a .417 batting average and seven RBIs that were compiled by his ten hits.

But the real story of the 1978 season, the tale of legend and folklore, took place not in the October classic but between July 17 and October 2.

The aforementioned "Zoo" was on full display in 1978 and, as the season wore on, was having an obvious effect on the team's ability to succeed, or even compete. Some attributed the Yankees' lackluster performance to Billy Martin. Others, probably more, held Reggie responsible, as Billy was, for the most part, adored by the fans. Still, others laid blame at the feet of George Steinbrenner, which is probably correct. Jackson may have been the straw that stirred the drink, but George was the gin, the vermouth, and the olives. The negative impact on the team was so debilitating that, by midseason, less than a week after the all-star game, the defending world champions sat a full fourteen games behind the rampaging Boston Red Sox.

Then, the apple cart that was the Yankees' 1978 season completely flipped over on July 17. In a game against the Red Sox at the stadium, the Billy-Reggie feud boiled over when Jackson ignored the hit-away sign after two failed attempts at bunting Thurman Munson from first to second. Reggie struck out, squaring around again in a futile third attempt. The next day, Reggie was suspended for five days without pay. Jackson flew home to the West Coast, and the Yankees moved on to Minnesota to play the Twins. Martin, who never needed much prompting to get fired up, was still hot about the incident and its aftermath. Jackson returned on July 23 and did not go back in the lineup immediately, but the verbal volleys associated with "buntgate" continued to play out to the delight of the press. After a July 23 win over the White Sox, Billy cozied up to the bar with some reporters and, with regard to Jackson and Steinbrenner, made the following remark: "One's a born liar, and one's convicted," alluding to

George's 1974 guilty plea related to illegal campaign contributions made to Richard Nixon's presidential campaign.

After George heard about Billy's remark, the die was cast and he "resigned" as Yankees manager the following day. By July 25, Bob Lemon, the even-tempered, veteran manager who had been fired by the White Sox about a month earlier came on board to, hopefully, steady the Yankees' ship.

To cap off this bizarre comedy of errors, on Old-Timers' Day, July 29, 1978, less than a week after Billy's departure, the Yankees announced that, in 1980, Lemon would move to the front office as general manager and Martin would return as manager. Billy was given a standing ovation. Reggie was booed. This was the first incarnation of the revolving-door saga that would play out between George and Billy and send Martin in and out of the Yankees dugout, five times over the next decade.

At the same time these seismic events were taking place in Yankeedom, a similar earth-shaking event was happening elsewhere. At first, it went somewhat unnoticed due to the circus that was occurring in the Bronx. But just about the same time the Yankees had hit bottom, the Red Sox started to collapse.

Between July 17 and September 6, there was a complete geomagnetic reversal of the American League East poles. Over that time, the Yankees went on a tear, 35-14. Boston, however, could barely top the .500 mark, going 25-24 over the same stretch. Do the math. As opposed to the volcanic-tempered Martin, the reserved and steady Lemon had skippered the team to within four games of the Red Sox just as the Bombers headed to Boston for a four-game series at Fenway.

What happened next is now chiseled into Yankees lore as nothing less than historic. While the press's labeling of what transpired that weekend as the "Boston Massacre" was a catchy and appropriate term for the ass-whooping the Yanks laid on the Sox, it was different from the original massacre of 1770 where British soldiers fired into a crowd of rowdy, snowball-throwing, obscenity hurling Bostonians. The colonial versions of, say, Patriots fans. Rather, it was a battlefield rout commensurate with some of the most iconic in world history. It was Napoleon at Austerlitz. It was Sitting Bull at Little Big Horn. It was Nick Faldo and Greg Norman at the 1996 Masters. During the series, the Yankees absolutely dismantled Red Sox pitching and hitting and outscored Boston 42-9 over the four, Thursday through Sunday, contests. In any event, when the smoke cleared on September 10, New York and Boston were tied atop the AL East.

While the Red Sox were certainly reeling (and embarrassed) by the spanking that occurred at Fenway, both teams knew that it was not quite a done deal yet. There were still twenty games left in the season. And, while the Yankees' lead extended to as much as three and a half games on September 17, although I am loath to give it, the Red Sox deserve some credit for not completely throwing in the towel as things started to get much tighter heading down the stretch.

In fact, even though New York finished the season winning six of eight, Boston did them two better by sweeping all of their games over the same time. This series of events culminated on October 1, 1978, when the Yankees dropped their last game to, of all teams, the 69-90 Cleveland Indians, while the Sox dispatched with the Toronto Blue Jays. The loss-win sequence on the last day of the season meant one thing: New York and Boston were, once again, tied for the AL East crown. In real terms, the result was that a one-game playoff was now necessary to determine who would go on to face Kansas City in the playoffs for the pennant. After a coin toss, won by the Red Sox, the game would be played at Fenway on Monday, October 2.

Like many of the memorable events chronicled in this book, I remember exactly where I was at the time of the playoff game. This was 1978, a year before I had ascended the departmental ranks at Pathmark to the frozen food department. On that October afternoon, I was working in the dairy section. I would end up working at Pathmark on three separate occasions, dairy, frozen foods, and even, for about a week, as a cart boy. Such was the nature of my teenage employment history as I can recount no fewer than eight different jobs I held over the two years between my sixteenth and eighteenth birthdays. This included working at the Scarsdale A&P, a trophy store, and a Chicken Delight franchise. At one time, Chicken Delight had been a significant competitor to Kentucky Fried Chicken in pre–Chick-fil-A and Popeye's America. During the biennium of my high school employment history, at one point or another, all of my friends and I worked for "Chicken Joe," proprietor, friend, and all-around goofball.

But on that October afternoon, in the days before bar codes, I was using my pricing gun and stocking milk, butter, cheese, and sour cream in the refrigerator cases all while keeping an ear open to the transistor radio on my table. Remember, this was still a time when playoff and World Series games were often played in the afternoon. Rather than a money grab for advertising dollars and increasing West Coast ratings, Major League Baseball played, and television covered, playoff series at times where kids could run home from school and catch the action before dinner, rather than after bedtime.

Of course, with everything on the line, the game was going to be stressful. With Ron Guidry pitching on only three days' rest, things got more precarious as Louisiana Lightning gave up two runs to Red Sox hitters. Meanwhile, Mike Torrez, refugee and traitor from the '77 Yanks and who won two games, including the clincher, in the series against the Dodgers, held the Bombers scoreless through six and two-thirds.

Free agency was what it was. Certainly the Yankees had taken advantage of the situation and profited from it. But what Torrez did, leave the Yankees and go immediately to the hated Red Sox, was inexcusable. It was more than my die-hard, teenage sensibilities could take. To me, he was Judas Iscariot. He was Benedict Arnold. *Et tu*, Torrez.

In the top of the seventh, back-to-back singles sandwiched in between two outfield flies had Torrez one out away from shutting the Yankees down in yet another inning. All he had to do was get the number nine hitter in the order out and move on to be within six outs of heading to the ALCS.

When shortstop Bucky Dent walked into the batter's box, there was, as there always is for die-hard fans, hope. However, if we were being honest, most Yankees fans were wishing someone else was at the plate at that moment. Dent, a solid-fielding shortstop had missed a decent portion of the season from a bruised shin that he had suffered from fouling a ball off of it. But Bucky was batting ninth in the lineup for a reason. His batting average in 1978 was a mediocre .243. Yet, as we know, baseball is the place for miracles to happen, and one of the greatest in baseball history was about to occur.

As Torrez wound up and delivered the ball, Bucky fouled the 1-0 pitch right off of his shin and immediately hit the dirt. Yankees trainer Gene Monahan came out to take a look at the grimacing Yankee. Monahan sprayed his lower shin area with a concoction, I think ethyl chloride, a mild anesthetic that seemed to be omnipresent on the baseball diamond whenever someone got nailed with a pitch or a line drive. After a minute or so, Dent stepped back in the batter's box. He took his practice swings. Since Bucky choked up so much, it looked like he was swinging about half of his bat and only a relatively small portion could actually make contact with the ball.

By this time, a small crowd of customers and employees had made their way around my table and were listening to the action on my transistor. Groups had done this throughout the day, popping their heads in when the Yanks appeared to be threatening. However, up until now, it always went for naught. This scene was replicated all around the store as other employees had also brought their radios with them.

In any event, Torrez threw the 1-1 pitch. Dent turned on it and got enough of his bat on it to send it high into the air. How high? The ball must've gone at least thirty-eight feet in the air and traveled at least 311 feet because all that Red Sox legendary left fielder Carl Yastrzemski could do was turn around and watch the ball as it sailed into the net above Fenway's Green Monster.

There was an immediate, spontaneous celebration in the dairy aisle between friends and strangers alike. Cheers could be heard through the store for the next few minutes. In fact, it carried on so long that I'm not sure many of us in the store noticed that, two batters later and after a pitching change, the Yanks had tacked on another run and now led 4-2. I know I didn't.

In the eighth, almost inconspicuously, Reggie Jackson launched one of his patented blasts to deep center field and the Yanks' lead was extended to three runs. As the song goes, it was all over but the crying. But the Red Sox had not come this far to simply lie down in front of their home crowd. In the bottom of the eighth, Goose Gossage, who had come on to relieve Guidry in the seventh, gave up two runs to tighten up the contest and Yankees fans' sphincters all over the tri-state area. The Bronx Bombers went down quietly in the top of the ninth. In the bottom of the inning, with everything on the line, two out and two Red Sox on base, Gossage got Carl Yastrzemski to pop the ball up in foul territory behind third base. The sure-handed Graig Nettles settled under it and squeezed the ball in his glove, and the celebration began. After an amazing roller coaster of a season, the Yankees were on the way, once again, to face off against the Royals for the pennant. As it had from time to time until the year 2004, the Curse of the Bambino had reared its head.

While the Bucky Dent homer is the moment that is most memorialized by fans and sports historians alike, many forget that Jackson's eighth inning blast was actually the difference in the game. Given the gravity of the moment and the unlikely hero in this case, perhaps it is warranted. No doubt Dent's three-run shot off of Torrez was historic. It reinvigorated the team and totally changed the dynamic of the game. It was Dent's blast above the Green Monster that became a thing of legend, but quietly it was Reggie who won the game.

As mentioned earlier, looking back, on some level, the '77 and '78 championships are indistinguishable. However, it is the road to those two titles that sets them apart from one another. The year 1977 was extremely satisfying as it was the first World Series title in a decade and a half: we had outlasted both the hated Orioles and Red Sox during the pennant race; we had dispatched with both the royal blue attired, obnoxious Royals and Dodgers; and, my guy, Reggie, had put on an unprecedented home run exhibition in game six and won the MVP award.

But despite the achievement of '77, 1978 will always have a slight edge in my book. With all of the clubhouse turmoil, including a midseason change in managers, the fourteen-game deficit, the Boston Massacre, the playoff game at Fenway, and a repeat against the same two loathsome franchises, the 1978 victory just tastes sweeter.

Chapter 11
Lumber and Lightning, "We Are Family," and Deja Vu All Over Again

I knew that my 1977 trip to Three Rivers would likely be my last game in person in the Steel City, at least for the Forgettable Decade. At the end of the summer, in September of 1977, I would turn sixteen years old, making me eligible to obtain what were referred to as "working papers," the documents that allowed high school kids the opportunity to go out and earn a few bucks for gas, beer, cassettes, and whatever else tickled their fancy. For me, however, working papers amounted to a get-out-of-jail-free card, for when 1978 rolled around, as with my sisters before me, once I became a viable member of the workforce, I was excused from the trek out to Republic.

As mentioned earlier, I recall little from that last Pirates game, other than the Bucs beat the Mets and the Son of Sam saga ended. I also have a vivid memory of the scorecard the Pirates put out that year.

The 1977 Bucs program featured cartoon drawings of players in action—running, hitting, and sliding in the different incarnations of uniforms that the team had adopted that year. Building on the previous slogan, "The Lumber Company," this team was supposed to combine the power of the early '70s team with speed on the base paths and was christened, "Lumber and Lightning."

Also, in a fit of what might be diagnosed as an acute case of *Whitesoxitis*, the Buccos, in 1977, adopted a cornucopia of uniform combinations, seven in all, which, depending on one's tastes, were brought forth to either excite or nauseate the fans.

I suppose, if you included amalgams of stirrups, undershirts, and caps, more combos could be put together. But the eclectic mix-and-match buffet of possible Pittsburgh uniform choices on any given day typically would look as follows:
- Black tops with gold pants and gold caps,
- Gold tops with black pants and black caps,
- White pinstriped tops and pants and black caps (home games only),
- Gold tops with gold pants and black caps,
- Black tops with black pants and gold caps, and the almost unimaginable,
- White pinstriped tops with black pants and gold caps, or,
- White pinstriped tops with yellow pants and black caps.

Unlike the Steelers, whose "Pittsburgh Gold" was actually a marigold and which, over the years, some of the uninitiated have mistakenly referred to the color as "yellow" (note to Wiz Khalifa). The Pirates, on the other hand, seemed to experiment with different shades of the gilded hue throughout the decade. In 1970, the Bucs were the first to don the pullover, beltless, double-knit uniforms that caught fire in the major leagues in the '70s, wearing white at home and gray on the road. In those days, Pirate "gold" resembled a kind of Gulden's mustard color. Eventually, the team transitioned to Steelers gold as the decade closed.

In 1976, the National League, celebrating their one-hundredth-year anniversary, adopted a pill box cap with piping, a literal tip of the hat to the nostalgic days of the 1870s. The Bucs, for an inexplicable reason, retained this chapeau through the 1970s and into the early '80s.

After a fabulous 1978 season for my teams, a Yankees World Series championship followed immediately with a Steelers Super Bowl, many, if not most fans would be content to sit back and bask in those victories. Given the infrequency of teams winning multiple world championships and dynastic dominance on the playing field, this tandem of titles could provide contentment for a long time. For some, bragging rights might last years. I didn't know it at the time, but as it turned out, my teams still had more gas left in the tank. As such, I was not looking for anything special in April of 1979 as the baseball season got underway. Besides, I had other things going on. In June, I would graduate from high school, and by late August I'd be heading off to my freshman year at college.

Also, the Yankees were never really a threat to three-peat in 1979. On June 1, the Bombers were still in it, three and one-half games behind the division-leading Orioles. By the end of the month, however, they trailed the Birds by twelve. In August, they had fallen to fourteen games back. 1978 would not replicate itself, and the Yankees would finish the season thirteen and a half games behind Baltimore, never having seriously contended for the pennant at any point.

The Pirates, however, were another matter entirely. From a baseball perspective, the Bucs' 1979 reemergence dovetailed nicely with the Yankees' back-to-back championships. After three years of watching the Phillies win in the NL East, the Pirates positioned themselves with an opportunity to make it back to the World Series altar in 1979. However, it was by no means a cakewalk.

For the early part of the 1979 season, the Pirates treaded water around .500. But in mid-May the team began a trend that can only be characterized as remarkable. Between May 16 and May 21, the Bucs ran off a six-game winning streak. This was the beginning of a recurrence that carried the team throughout the season and into the playoffs. Nine times during the season, the Pirates boasted winning streaks of four or more games, including nine consecutive wins from July 14 to July 23. The Pirates amassed fifty-five wins during these runs, a total of 56 percent of their victories. If you roll three-game winning streaks into the mix, the number jumps to seventy games, or 71.4 percent. That means the Buccos sprinkled only twenty-eight wins over the course of ninety-two games in 1979. The rest came in chunks of three to nine games.

In addition to the Lumber and Lightning moniker, the Pirates and their fans also coalesced around a Grammy-nominated song that became an anthem for the team as they navigated through the season, the playoffs, and the World Series. Sister Sledge, the Pennsylvania-born (albeit from Philadelphia) quartet's 1979 hit single, "We Are Family," became omnipresent at Three Rivers and was formally adopted throughout Pirate Country after a five-run, ninth-inning, walk-off victory over the Padres on June 1.

As the season drew to a close, on September 15 the Pirates were one half game behind the Montreal Expos. By September 29, the Pirates had jumped ahead in the standings and led the Expos by one game. The season ended on September 30, 1979, with the Pirates beating the Cubs in their 162nd game of the year. The win was critical as the Expos dropped their 160th game to the Phillies that same day, giving the Pirates a two-game edge and the NL East title. During the year, the Expos and Atlanta Braves had two contests rained out. If the Pirates had finished only one game ahead (i.e., lost to the Cubs), the Expos would have traveled to Atlanta for a doubleheader to make up the two rainouts. An Expos sweep of the Braves would then have forced a one-game playoff with the Buccos as both teams would have finished the season with 97-65 records. But, as my mother would sometimes say, "If ifs and ands were pots and pans, there'd be no need for tinkers," and the Pirates' 5-3 win over the Cubs made the scenario moot. My friend Moose had a similar, but less genteel, saying that communicated the same sentiment: "If the queen had balls, she'd be king."

However, despite the euphoria over the Pirates' reascension to prominence, a major stumbling block lay in the way. Before the Bucs could earn their way back to the World Series, they had to overcome a significant obstacle. A Big Red hurdle.

The Reds finished atop the NL West division, winning ninety games and, like the Pirates, squeaked by their closest rival, the second-place Houston Astros that finished a game and a half back. The Pirates won ninety-eight games that year and looked like the better team on paper, but there was too much history between these two franchises that made their homes on the banks of the Ohio River. The ghosts of 1970, 1972, and 1975 still lingered. When the Pirates won the World Series in 1971, they beat the San Francisco Giants for the pennant, not the Reds, who had finished a dismal fourth that year, eleven games behind the Giants. But in sports, opportunities at redemption and overcoming the ghosts of playoffs past are what make the game worth watching.

The Lumber and Lightning moniker was not the only difference from their earlier Lumber Company counterparts. The '79 squad was also different in appearance. The only Buccos left from the 1971 championship roster were Stargell, who had become dean of Pirates baseball and had moved from left field to first base, and Rennie Stennett, who split time between second base and the outfield in '71, and spent about half of the 1979 season as the starting second baseman. But Stennett sat out the other half in favor of Phil Garner who was part of a quintet of infielders, along with Stennett, Tim Foli, Bill Madlock, and Dale Berra who platooned the second-base, shortstop, and third-base duties.

The third member of the '71 championship team was Manny Sanguillén, who, at age thirty-five, was reduced to eighty at bats during the season and only occasionally squatted behind the dish, spelling the full-time catching tandem of Ed Ott and Steve Nicosia.

Finally, there was Dock Ellis. Ellis had been traded from the team in 1976 and made the rounds between the Yankees, A's, Rangers, and Mets before landing back in the Steel City at the end of September. Sanguillén had only three at bats in the fall classic, Stennett one, with two hits between them. Ellis did not make the World Series roster.

The Clementes and Al Olivers of the era had been replaced with the likes of Bill "Mad Dog" Madlock and Dave "the Cobra" Parker. Madlock, who had stints with the Cubs and the Giants, was one of the players involved in the trade that sent Bobby Murcer from San Francisco to Chicago. Mad Dog would win four batting titles over his career—two with the Pirates. Parker, the cannon-armed right fielder, was consistently near the top of NL batting statistics and garnered two of his own batting titles while with the Bucs. Add Willie Stargell and his two NL home run titles to the mix, and Lumber and Lightning was formidable.

On the other hand, the Reds, other than the pitching staff, which now boasted Tom Seaver, had an almost identical lineup to their 1976 World Series team, albeit a bit longer in the tooth. The stage, therefore, was now set for either redemption or continued heartbreak.

This time, however, there would be no Johnny Bench homer or wild pitch to dash the hopes of Pirates fans as had been done earlier in the decade. This time, the Buccos ousted the Reds in four games, transforming the Big Red Machine into nothing more than a little red wagon. It was glorious!

With the Reds dispatched and the ghosts of failed NLCSs past dismissed, one more specter remained on the horizon. In 1979, like the Pirates, the Baltimore Orioles had returned from their stint in baseball purgatory. Having won the American League East, between 1969, the onset of divisional play, until the end of 1974, the Birds won the division five out of six times. In many ways, like the Pirates, despite this success, the O's fell short of expectations. During that early '70s run, the team lost in two of its three World Series appearances (1969 and 1971) and were defeated in the ALCS in their other two pennant runs (1973 and 1974). So, in a way, I could relate to Orioles fans. However, as the Yankees' main nemesis in the first half of the decade, I hated the Orioles. So, while I can relate, I didn't care.

The venue for the 1979 postseason was unique for me. It would not be spent in the bosom of my family at my ancestral home on Candlewood Drive. Rather, it would be spent on the First East floor at Tobey Hall at the State University of New York (SUNY) College at Oneonta.

Many, if not most kids from my area, never thought about going anywhere but to a SUNY school. Some of the really bright students might end up at an Ivy League or a Colgate or a Brandeis, but they were few and far between. SUNY schools were affordable, and these were the days when colleges and universities resembled educational institutions, rather than competitive arenas for children to be used for Baby Boomer and Gen X parents to compete with their friends and neighbors for bragging rights. Therefore, affordability was paramount. For the most part, SUNY schools were a given.

The SUNY system was made up of an archipelago of two- and four-year colleges and a handful of university centers, mostly scattered throughout the vastness of upstate New York. I'm sure everyone had their own opinion, but I felt that Oneonta was the best option as it was reasonably close to home (three hours from Yonkers); I knew a decent amount of people who went or were going there; it was located about a half hour from Cooperstown and the Baseball Hall of Fame; purportedly, the ratio of girls to guys was 5:1; and, legend had it, there were fifty-two bars in the town. The latter two points may have gotten me over the finish line in terms of the decision-making process. It was also said that the college had a very good baseball team and, originally, I was intent on extending my playing career beyond high school.

Attending Oneonta was also preferable to ending up at one of the SUNY schools located either at the edge of the known universe (Oswego,

Plattsburgh, Potsdam), or in some jerkwater town where nothing of remote interest was happening (Fredonia, Cobleskill, Delhi). Oneonta was merely backwater, not jerkwater.

Tobey Hall was one of the older dorms on campus, a rectangular building with three floors divided into east and west wings. My floor, First East, was all guys. Second and Third East, all girls. First West was all girls too, and I have no memory of who or what sex lived on the two floors above them. Given that 5:1 ratio thing, it may have been more girls. There was a lower level that was only above ground in the rear of the dorm and, therefore, had a limited number of rooms. "The Pit," as it was called, I believe was all guys.

First East was an amalgam of "wet behind the ears" freshmen and juniors that were hardened veterans of campus life. There were a few sophomores thrown into the mix as well. Perhaps transfers and refugees from other schools.

Welcoming me to First East and assisting me in the lost sheep syndrome that many freshmen experience when becoming a stranger in a strange land was another Roosevelt High grad, Ed Young. Eddie was two years my elder and played first base ahead of me on the Indians baseball team. Since I was one of only two sophomores that made the varsity, he was an on-the-field mentor to me, teaching me some of the tricks of the trade and expanding my acumen for playing the anchor position on the right side of the infield. But despite this positive turn of events upon entering my new living quarters, my introduction to my new roommate would be an entirely different matter.

Entering room 108 for the first time with my parents, I met my dorm compatriot, Neal Saperstein. Neal was in the room with his friend Dave, who lived in the Pit. Their eyes were bloodshot, and the room reeked of pot. Strike one. My friends and I were athletes. We were beer drinkers. We viewed most pot smokers (at least the ones in Roosevelt that we weren't friends with) as Heads or Druggies. Oddly, the group I got to know and hang out with at Tobey Hall had a similar philosophy. While we were not Oneonta athletes, we were athletic, participating in intramural football and floor hockey, working out at the gym, and spending more time on recreational activities than we did studying.

Neal and Dave extended their hands, not in the regular handshake position, but with wrists cocked upward in the style that hippies had co-opted from Black guys in the 1960s. This was an early form of social gentrification that was accompanied by the query, "What's up, man?" Strike two. As I put my bags down in the room and looked at the wall above my new roommate's bed, I saw three posters: the Grateful Dead, New Riders of the Purple Sage, and Hot Tuna. Strike three.

It wasn't that Neal Saperstein was a bad guy. Quite the opposite. We were just oil and water. We traveled in different circles. Ships that passed neither in the day nor in the night. Neal was an early riser. I was a night owl. He would be off to class while I was still sleeping. When he returned, I was at class. After that, he hung out with his friends and I hung out with mine. By October, a room had opened up on the floor, and I moved in with one of my new friends, one of a trio of guys from Massapequa, Long Island, who had been tripled up with his two high school pals. Saperstein moved down to the Pit with his boys. Ours was a friendship that was simply not meant to be.

My new roommate, Tim Hanin, was, however, like no other Jewish kid I had ever met. For starters, he was big and burly, huge in both height and girth. He had what sounded like an Irish last name. He drank like the Irish guys I grew up with too. He was not a particularly good student, and he loved sports. Perhaps he was a descendant of the house of Dan, one of the lost tribes of Israel that some believe ended up on the Emerald Isle.

Rounding out my inventory of new dorm mates, along with Hanin's two former roommates, the aforementioned members of the Massapequa Mafia, was one Italian and one Jewish kid from Brooklyn, my new junior pals, who I met through Eddie Young, and at the far end of the hall were Sam and Bob. I believe two of the sophomores that inhabited the floor.

Sam was a gregarious type who, I remember, had heterochromia (i.e., two different colored eyes, one brown eye and one blue). On the other hand, Bob, with his homochromatic peepers, was about as quiet a person as they come. As my first semester moved forward, and the 1979 fall classic approached, it became known that Bob was a Baltimore Orioles fan. I am not sure what he or his family had done to have this pox bestowed upon their house, but for God's sake, Bob was from upstate New York, not the Delmarva Peninsula! Perhaps he had spent his youth experiencing dysfunctional summer vacations on the Chesapeake Bay. In any event, at the outset of the series, he was, like most of America, extremely confident about the O's chances. The ten-dollar bet we made ($42.38 in today's dollars), from his perspective, seemed to be money in the bank.

As the World Series progressed, Bob's confidence grew stronger, especially when the heavily favored Orioles jumped out to a three-games-to-one lead. This included beating Pittsburgh in game four at Three Rivers and overcoming a 6-3 deficit by scoring six runs in the eighth and thwarting the Bucs' chance to tie up the series. The Orioles now stood at the precipice of victory much to the despair of the Pirate faithful. After that game, I may have felt down and out, but the Pirates weren't finished. Between October 14 and October 17, over the next three games, the Pirates made history.

During this last act of the 1979 season, the Bucs outscored Baltimore 15-2, including a 7-1 game five rout in Pittsburgh and dominating the last two contests played on the road at Memorial Stadium. In doing so, they became only the fourth team in the annals of seven-game World Series play to overcome a three-games-to-one deficit and the first since 1968. Just like 1971, the Pirates had stunned the sports world, their critics, and, most importantly, the Orioles!

Other storylines that came out of the 1979 series were tales of both redemption and achievement that exorcized the demons for some of the Pirates players and myself alike.

First, Grant Jackson, the Yankees pitcher that gave up that three-run homer to George Brett in game five of the 1976 ALCS, came to the mound in relief, blanked the Birds over two and two-thirds innings, and got the win in a dramatic game seven in Baltimore.

Kent Tekulve, who had served up the bottom of the ninth home run to Lee Mazzilli in 1976 at the infamous leave-early game, notched three saves in the series, again, including game seven.

Willie Stargell, who I had watched and admired throughout the Forgettable Decade, was named World Series MVP. Papa Stargell batted .267 with eight RBIs and three homers, including a massive two-run blast in the sixth inning of game seven that gave the Pirates the lead and turned out to be the game winner.

The Pirates' World Series win on October 17, 1979, bookended their 1971 title and dovetailed nicely into the Steelers midseason run at a fourth Super Bowl title. Following the Bucs' win over the Orioles, the Steelers added onto a 5-2 record and went on a four-game winning streak on the way to a 12-4 overall record and the AFC Central title, as they had for the last six years and seven out of the last eight seasons.

Time was running out on the Forgettable Decade, but it was looking as though the '70s would end with a bang. In fact, the 1978–1979 run of my sports teams, two World Series and two Super Bowl championships in succession, barring some odd combination of team love and with similar geographic ties, would be hard for anyone to match. I just haven't met any lifelong Blue Jays/Cowboys fans from the early nineties. Then again, why would I want to?

Chapter 12
Cementing the Dynasty—Super Bowls XIII and XIV

Coming off the Super Bowl X victory over Dallas, anticipation was again high in the Steel City with talk of a three-peat. The rumblings about this third consecutive Lombardi trophy, however, were quickly silenced as the season began to unfold. Late-game defensive collapses and inconsistency by, and injuries to, Terry Bradshaw, including the infamous Turkey Joe Jones incident that knocked Bradshaw senseless in week five against Cleveland, left the Black and Gold staring into a regular season abyss at 1-4 with more than a third of the season already gone. Perhaps, a back-to-back Lombardi Trophy drinking binge had taken its toll on the Steel Curtain and led to a hangover.

But seven days later something happened. Whether it was self-examination, pride, or just growing tired of sportswriters and commentators delivering premature obituaries for the 1976 season, the Steelers, led almost entirely by the defense, regrouped and put on one of the greatest performances in NFL history over the remaining nine games.

Resurrected, the Steelers ran the table for the balance of the '76 season, allowing opponents to score only twenty-eight points over that stretch of games. If defenses that do not yield a lot of points are called stingy, the Steel Curtain was downright miserly. They were Ebenezer Scrooge on December 23, the day before Marley showed up. When I say, "led almost entirely by the defense," I mean it. Bradshaw's backup, Mike Kruczek, did not exactly light up the scoreboard during his six-win, no-loss stretch until number twelve's return.

Perhaps the most astounding statistic regarding that 1976 defense was that over those nine games, the Steel Curtain shut out their opponents five times, a record in the modern era that still stands today. The shutout performance exhibited such a stifling of their opponents' offensive production that it would've impressed the likes of contemporary shutout standouts, the MLB's Bob Gibson and the NHL's Tony Esposito.

Kruczek was one of those players that was a college prodigy and an all-American at Boston College that did almost nothing in his pro career except being in the room when they handed out the rings for Super Bowls XIII and XIV. As a quarterback taking up space on the Pittsburgh sideline over four years, Kruczek threw for a total of 976 yards, zero touchdowns, and six interceptions. The bulk of these statistics were compiled while at the helm in 1976, including the zero touchdowns. He did, however, rush for two TDs during his 6-0 stretch.

The Black and Gold maintained this momentum right into the playoffs. However, because of their early season foibles, the Steelers found themselves having to play on the road instead of in the comfort of Three Rivers Stadium. Based on final records, the number three-seeded Steelers would have to travel to Baltimore to play the formerly great, and recently rejuvenated, Colts.

I remember that game very well for one reason. Played on December 19, I watched the game as we were putting the final touches on our Christmas tree decorations. The color television was located downstairs in the den, so I watched the game in the living room, on a small black-and-white TV my older sister had been given when she went off to college and which had somehow made its way back into our, meaning my, possession. Even though I had to watch the Steelers slap around the Colts on a twelve-inch, black-and-white screen, it was supremely enjoyable as the Steelers, not known for jumping out to big leads, bested the Colts by halftime, 26-7, and never looked back en route to a 40-14 win. But the victory at Memorial Stadium was pyrrhic. Both Franco Harris and Rocky Bleier were injured in the game, meaning Pittsburgh would have to go to the AFC championship game without their ball-controlling, clock-consuming duo of thousand-yard rushers.

The win set up, for the third year in a row, an AFC championship game matchup versus the hated Raiders. Since Oakland had the best record in the entire league that year at 13-1, an injured, depleted Pittsburgh would again have to travel. However, if there was hope to be had, the day before the win against the Colts, Oakland had barely squeaked by the wild card, New England Patriots, 24-21, in a game that was viewed, except by, I suppose, the Raider faithful, as having been horribly officiated. Since they have been the recipients of so many referee-friendly calls since 2000, I will leave any discussion about unfairness in the 1976 playoffs for Patriots fans. They are, without doubt, experts on the subject.

Since this is a book about *fond memories,* I will not bore the reader or torture myself with a recap of that game, otherwise to say, without Harris and Bleier, it was excruciating. Forced to rely almost totally on the passing game into a Raiders secondary that could just sit back and rub their grubby little hands together lying in wait for Steelers receivers, the Raiders jumped out to a 17-7 halftime lead. After that, Oakland only had to scrimmage with Pittsburgh through the second half on their way to a 24-7 win and, ultimately, a victory against the Vikings in Super Bowl XI.

And so, a championship game three-peat against Oakland and in the Super Bowl was not in the cards that year. As for the Raiders, the

Black and Gold and the Silver and Black would not meet again in the playoffs for the balance of the Forgettable Decade. Going forward to today, the only time the two teams have met in the postseason was in the 1983 season, when Los Angeles, not Oakland, was on their way to their third Super Bowl title.

The bitter rivalry that was forged between Pittsburgh and Oakland in the 1970s was put on indefinite hold, recurring twenty-one times over the next fifty years, rarely at critical moments in the regular season, except, maybe, for Steelers and Raiders fans. As for the 1976 playoff loss, it was painful, as are all losses to the Raiders. I didn't like it, but maybe it was just their year.

If 1976 was a promising yet disappointing season, 1977 was another matter entirely. The off-season was fraught with player contract disputes, litigation, and other controversy. The inevitable fruits of success, I guess.

Although the Steelers won the AFC Central again that year, it was only with a record of 9-5, last among the other playoff teams, including the Raiders, who entered the playoffs as the wild card with a much stronger record of 11-3. Therefore, it was no great surprise when the Steel Curtain was sent to the showers early in the divisional round by the eventual conference champs, the Denver Broncos. This was the first time the Black and Gold had been dispatched before the championship round since 1973.

Of course, this sucked, but the Yankees had just come off their first World Series victory in fifteen years, and pitchers and catchers were only about two months away, making for an upcoming 1978 baseball season that looked pretty encouraging. Therefore, even as a rabid sports fan, one must not get too greedy, especially with three of my best friends having been Raiders, Vikings, and Cowboys fans, teams that the Steelers had laid waste to in recent years.

In 1978, the Steelers reemerged as top contenders for the AFC crown. However, their main competition was the Houston Oilers, who, by the end of the Forgettable Decade, had surpassed the Raiders as our most competitive rivals. The Oilers, however, were immensely more likable than the hated Raiders. Led by ten-gallon, Stetson chapeau–wearing head coach Bum Philips, a strong defense, a paesano of a quarterback named Dan Pastorini, and one of my favorite running backs to ever play the game, Earl Campbell, the Oilers were formidable.

The Oilers had a motto, "Luv Ya Blue," which their fans would brandish on placards and wave around enthusiastically at home games. They even had a song, one that they had co-opted from the Miami Dolphins and transformed into a cornball, yet listenable ditty. The first verse went as follows:

Look out football, here we come,
Houston Oilers, number one.
Houston has the Oilers, the greatest football team
We take the ball from goal to goal like no one's ever seen
We're in the air, we're on the ground, always in control
And when you say the Oilers, you're talking Super Bowl
'Cause we're the Houston Oilers, Houston Oilers, Houston Oilers, Number
One.
Yes, we're the Houston Oilers, Houston Oilers, Houston Oilers, Number
One.

Campbell was a huge, powerful back out of the University of Texas and the 1977 Heisman Trophy winner. He had thighs like sequoia trunks and was an absolute terror to tackle, especially if he reached the secondary, and horrified cornerbacks and safeties had to try and wrap their arms around his massive, pistonlike thighs. Lost to the age of big, explosive offenses and the NFL Competition Committee, today, backs like Earl Campbell are, basically, extinct. At best, they are certainly on the endangered species list. Once and a while, a power runner is identi-fied in the wilds of the college ranks and makes an appearance in league play. I believe this is why we love the Derrick Henrys of this world. *Note to Steelers: looking back, maybe you should have kept LeGarrette Blount and jettisoned Le'Veon Bell in 2014. For God's sake, his name was Blount!*

Generally, it was always a bit unsettling when the Steelers got into one of their one-and-done playoff situations, except maybe against a team like the Baltimore Colts. However, against Campbell's legs, Pastori-ni's arm, and Billy "White Shoes" Johnson's feet, things got a little more precarious toward the end of the Forgettable Decade as, while the Steelers were still having success, there was concern that they were aging.

But, while the Oilers may have been up and coming, they were no match for the wrecking machine that the experienced and battle-test-ed Steelers had become. Pittsburgh finished the season 14-2, avenged their 1977 divisional loss to the Denver Broncos, 33-10, routed the Oil-ers 34-5 at the early one o'clock game on championship Sunday, and reestablished their dominance over the AFC.

On that same championship Sunday, the 4:00 p.m. game was also a decisive victory for the NFC team that would face off against the Steel-ers in Super Bowl XIII. After completely dismantling their opponents on offense, defense, special teams, cheerleader roster, and parking lot tailgate parties, the Cowboys' 28-0 shutout over the Los Angeles Rams set up a rematch of Super Bowl X, the first for the Lombardi Trophy since the creation of the contest a dozen years earlier.

Of course Super Bowl XIII brought with it the same emotions that came with Super Bowl X. Excitement, anticipation, nervousness, anxiety, and hatred for the fucking Cowboys. To the general sports world, the contest was seen as the battle of champions, a clash between the two premier franchises of the decade. In the aftermath, many continue to view the game as the greatest Super Bowl ever played. However, at the time and on paper, the two teams did not look much different than they did in Super Bowl X.

For Pittsburgh, the Steel Curtain, notwithstanding a few changes here and there, was intact. On offense, Bradshaw, Franco, Bleier, Swann, and Stallworth continued to lead the charge. The same could almost be said for the Cowboys—almost. While the majority of Doomsday was still on the defensive side of the ball, and Staubach, Robert Newhouse, and Drew Pearson continued to be offensive staples, there was one addition to the Dallas roster that made Steelers fans nervous.

Tony Dorsett had been the Cowboys' first pick in the 1976 draft. Born just north of the Steel City and playing his college ball at the University of Pittsburgh, he was another one of those products of western Pennsylvania that got away. A standout at Pitt, Dorsett won the 1976 Heisman Trophy, no pun intended, running away. Upon his arrival to the pros, Dorsett made his presence felt immediately and established himself as both a powerful runner up the middle and a speedy back that could also get around the end. He was an elusive runner that was tough to bring down in the open field and a double threat that could also be a weapon in the passing game. In his first season, he was named NFL Offensive Rookie of the Year. As it turned out, the Steel Curtain would have their hands full with Dorsett all game.

There was one additional difference between Super Bowl X and XIII that was not a result of moves made in the front office, on the sidelines, or in the draft and turned out to be more impactful than any changes to rosters might have. In fact, it took place prior to the first snap of the 1978 season.

In order to open up the offensive game and, ostensibly, to make the game more exciting, the NFL owners, through the Competition Committee, made some significant adjustments. Paramount among these was the transformational rule that defensive players could only hit a receiver within five yards of the line of scrimmage. Any contact beyond that point could be cited by the officials as either defensive holding or, if the contact occurred while the ball was in air, pass interference.

Perhaps the player that was most adept at, and had the biggest reputation for harassing, befuddling and generally beating on receivers as they entered their respective pass patterns was the Steelers' Mel Blount. Certainly Blount's stifling style of play was on the minds of the Competition Committee when adopting the new rule.

The six-foot-three, 211-pound, All-Pro cornerback looked like Isaac Hayes in shoulder pads and was not much smaller than the Steelers' linebacker corps of Lambert (six-foot-four, 220), Jack Ham (six-foot-one, 225), and Robin Cole (six-foot-two, 220). It is, therefore, no surprise that the league's new policy aimed at keeping receivers' heads attached to their shoulders and that drastically altered the interactions between pass catchers and defenders would be dubbed, "The Blount Rule."

The first quarter of Super Bowl XIII started out much like its predecessor, albeit as a negative image of the other. Early in Super Bowl X, Steelers punter Bobby Walden's muffed snap led to the first score of the game as Roger Staubach quickly cashed in on the foible with a touchdown pass to Drew Pearson. This time, it was Pearson who coughed up the ball near midfield, and shortly thereafter Bradshaw found wide receiver John Stallworth in the end zone giving Pittsburgh the early lead. And, like the 1975 contest, by the end of the first quarter, the two teams were knotted at seven points apiece. Except for one instance, much later in the game, that is where the similarities end.

The rest of the first half would set the tone for the balance of the game. With the offenses opened up, both Doomsday and the Steel Curtain would no longer be able to shut down the opponent and stuff the line of scrimmage. Moving forward, Super Bowl XIII would be a battle of big plays on offense and splash plays on defense.

For Dallas, two Bradshaw turnovers while being sacked led to two Cowboy touchdowns. One, a thirty-nine-yard pass from Staubach to Tony Hill and the other, a thirty-seven-yard touchdown jaunt by linebacker Mike Hegman after recovering a Bradshaw fumble.

For the Steelers, in addition to the Pearson fumble recovery that led to the first score, Mel Blount stepped in front of a Staubach pass just on the south side of the two-minute warning, giving the Black and Gold one more chance to put points on the board before the half. Six plays later, a seven-yard touchdown pass to Rocky Bleier garnered that score. The Bleier catch would be memorialized on the cover of *Sports Illustrated's* January 29, 1979, issue showing Rocky leaping into the air and falling backward into the end zone in front of Cowboy linebacker D. D. Lewis, who was sporting one of those "oh shit" looks on his face. Sandwich in a seventy-five-yard bomb from Bradshaw to Stallworth early in the second quarter, and the first thirty minutes of the battle of the champions ended with the score, Steelers 21, Cowboys 14.

The third quarter started out as a chess match with both teams trading punts until about halfway through the stanza. With about seven and a half minutes left in the quarter, and after a mediocre punt by Steelers' Craig Colquitt, Dallas went to work around midfield. A six-play, thirty-two-yard drive found the Cowboys with a third and three on the Steelers' ten-yard line. Staubach dropped back and found a wide-open Jackie Smith in the end zone only to have the play end with the ball rolling around on the painted turf. Dallas would have to settle for a field goal, Steelers 21, Dallas 17.

To this day, Cowboy fans continue to whine about how the dropped Jackie Smith pass was so devastating and that, had the future Hall of Famer reeled in the pass, we would have been looking at the first overtime Super Bowl game rather than another defeat at the hands of the Steel Curtain. However, the Smith drop came with almost three minutes remaining in the third quarter. Pittsburgh would go on to score two touchdowns over the next eleven minutes; therefore, it is impossible for one to extrapolate. Besides, from this fan's perspective, although the pass hit Smith in the hands and should have been caught (a cardinal tenet of armchair quarterbacking), the big tight end was going to the ground to make the catch of a low thrown ball. The pass was also thrown behind Smith.

While Cowboy fans obsess over the Jackie Smith drop as the turning point of the game, they are mistaken. Too much happened after the play, a combined thirty-one points scored by the two teams down the stretch of the game, the need for and execution of the onside kicks, et cetera. I could easily say that if Roy Gerela's field goal attempt, instead of hitting the upright back in the second quarter, had gone through, the game would have been out of reach. This is a common mistake made by fans on the losing side of a close game. The premise is, if *this* had happened instead of *that*, and everything else unfolded as it did, the outcome would have been different. It is a flawed theory. I have been guilty of falling into this trap many times over the years.

In the end, the truth is the momentum in Super Bowl XIII turned in much the same way it did in Super Bowl X. In that first contest, the Steelers comeback was ignited when Cliff Harris taunted Roy Gerela after a missed field goal and Jack Lambert was forced to spank the Dallas defender in front of a national television audience by tossing him to the turf. Similarly, the real turning point of the rematch at the Orange Bowl came as a result of another dick move by a Cowboy player.

With the Steelers leading 21-17 and facing a third and four at the Dallas seventeen with just over eight minutes to play, whistles blew as Bradshaw could not get the snap off in time. Despite the flag being thrown, resident douchebag Hollywood Henderson of Super Bowl X opening kickoff fame burst through the line, wrapped up Bradshaw, and threw him to the ground. The officials did not penalize Henderson for the dead ball hit, probably feeling that, because of the crowd noise, Henderson did not hear the whistle. Plus, it was the seventies.

Hollywood may not have heard the whistle, but Franco Harris did. The usually even-tempered Franco got into Henderson's face and made it clear he didn't appreciate the hit on his quarterback. As Bradshaw tells it, when the team got into the huddle, Harris asked, no, insisted on getting the ball.

Facing a third and nine, a clear passing situation, the Steelers came to the line and ran one of their patented trap plays instead. The Pittsburgh offensive line blew a hole in the center of the Cowboy defense the size of the Rio Grande. Franco exploded through the gap and romped twenty-two yards into the end zone. Steelers 28, Cowboys 17.

On the ensuing kickoff, Gerela slipped as he booted the ball, sending a squibbed knuckleball low and down the middle of the field that only reached the Dallas up men in the kickoff formation, basically the wedge blockers. Randy White, the Cowboys All-Pro and future Hall of Fame defensive lineman, scooped up the ball. But White had a cast on his hand due to a broken thumb. The clumsy, club-handed White lost control of the ball as he was hit by Tony Dungy. The pigskin was then pounced on by Steelers special teamer and reserve linebacker and proprietor of one of the best nicknames in NFL history, Dennis "Dirt" Winston. The recovery gave Pittsburgh the ball at the Dallas eighteen-yard line. One play later, Bradshaw hit Lynn Swann in the end zone, further extending the Pittsburgh lead to a monumental eighteen points with only about seven minutes left in the game. Only eleven seconds after the White fumble, Pittsburgh seemingly put the game out of reach with what would be the winning score.

I was euphoric. I was giddy. With such little time left on the clock and the two-point conversion being more than a decade and a half away, Dallas would need three touchdowns in the scant time remaining in order to pull out a victory. It was over. It was done. Even if Dallas were to drive for a score, it would still leave them two touchdowns shy with little time on the clock. But, as is their want, the Steelers felt compelled on some level to make the game competitive.

Like Super Bowl X, the Cowboys mounted a ferocious comeback that once again tightened the sphincters of Steelers fans but ultimately fell short.

After the Swann touchdown, Staubach and the Cowboys mounted an eight-play, eighty-nine-yard drive that pulled the team to within eleven points. However, the drive covered almost four minutes, leaving Dallas two touchdowns behind with just under three minutes left.

Of course, the Cowboys recovered the onside kick, leaving Steelers fans shaking their heads and rubbing the tops of their diaphragms from the agita that only their beloved team can inflict on them. The Cowboys would strike one more time, pulling within four points. But this final drive, which included an eleven-yard sack of Staubach by L. C. Greenwood, left America's Team with little time to do anything else. When Staubach hit Butch Johnson in the end zone to make the score 35-31, only twenty-six ticks remained on the game clock.

The last attempt at a miracle, another onside kick, was gobbled up by Rocky Bleier. Two fall downs by Bradshaw later (these were the days before the kneel), and it was all over.

◆◆◆

As with 1978, the Steelers once again squared off against the Houston Oilers for the AFC crown. During the late '70s, as a divisional and playoff opponent, the Oilers would have to be dealt with three times in a season—a sort of sneak peak of what would transpire a quarter century later with future Steelers-Ravens clashes.

The '79 AFC championship, however, played in frigid conditions at Three Rivers would not be a blowout like the prior year's contest. The scrappy Oilers trailed at the half only by a single score, 17-10. Pastorini, despite taking a tremendous beating from the Steel Curtain that day, refused to fold up his team's tent and attempted a late, second-half comeback.

A key moment came at the very end of the third quarter when the Houston quarterback hit wide receiver Mel Renfro, who gathered in Pastorini's pass as he slid out of the back of the end zone. Renfro was clearly inbounds, but the official's view was blocked by cornerback Ron Johnson, who had tight coverage on the play. Instant replay was not in use at the time, and, after a lengthy discussion, the referee ruled it an incomplete pass.

Like the Immaculate Reception and the Jackie Smith dropped touchdown, the Renfro nontouchdown call would have Houston fans joining the Oakland and Dallas faithful in the boo-hoo chorus: "We would've won if it wasn't for the refs."

Yes, the refs blew an obvious touchdown and forced Houston to settle for a field goal, making the score 17-13 instead of a tie game with about fifteen minutes left to play. But there were also a lot of other things the refs *didn't* do.

The refs didn't allow Pittsburgh to conduct two long, time-consuming, fourth-quarter drives leading to another ten points. Neither did the officials stuff Earl Campbell at the line of scrimmage, holding a 1,697-yard rusher to fifteen yards on the ground in seventeen tries. Nor did they force the Oilers to turn the ball over three times. The Steel Curtain did that. Final score: Steelers 27, Oilers 13.

Now, for the fourth time in six years, the Black and Gold was Super Bowl bound. Their opponents this time, the Los Angeles Rams, had won the NFC West every year between 1973 and 1979. The Rams, however, were perennial bridesmaids, consistently catching the NFC playoff bouquet but left at the altar by more powerful Cowboys and Vikings teams that dominated the decade and appeared in every NFL championship game and all but one Super Bowl between the 1969 and 1978 seasons.

If the Vikings, now losers of four Super Bowls, were consistently the place horse in the league's biggest contests during the 1970s, the Rams were the also-rans. For Los Angeles fans, the litany of losses reads like a "Who's Not Who" list of playoff disappointments:

- 1973, NFC divisional round, Dallas 27, Los Angeles 16
- 1974, NFC championship game, Minnesota 14, Los Angeles 10
- 1975, NFC championship game, Dallas 37, Los Angeles 7
- 1976, NFC championship game, Minnesota 24, Los Angeles 13
- 1977, NFC divisional round, Minnesota 14, Los Angeles 7

In 1978, the Rams beat the Vikings 34-10 in the divisional round but were shut out by the Cowboys in the NFC championship game, 28-0.

In 1979, however, the Rams finally exorcised their demons by defeating the Cowboys, 21-19, in the divisional round of the playoffs at Texas Stadium. They then went on to beat the creamsicle-clad Tampa Bay Buccaneers, 9-0, in the conference championship, giving them the opportunity to take on the Steel Curtain in Pasadena at the Rose Bowl and only a hop, skip, and jump from their Los Angeles Coliseum home turf.

Super Bowl XIV was unique, however, in that, unlike all previous Black and Gold stressful experiences, I wasn't worried at all about a possible Steelers loss. I was, in fact, supremely confident going into the game. Perhaps, it was the Rams' reputation as losers of big games. Maybe, it was the atmosphere in which I saw the game. I watched Super Bowl XIV in Oneonta in the Tobey Hall common room, as I had just returned to college from Christmas break. I was also sporting a cast on my left hand.

In January of 1980, while on Christmas vacation. I broke my hand, my left hand to be exact, in a bar fight at a local dive in Mount Vernon, called the Cedarcrest. It was the type of watering hole that we frequented quite often because it was around the corner from a local disco called Hoops and the drinks were cheaper. Also, we could get a bit of a respite from all of the hairspray, perfume, cologne, and gold chains (on the guys, of course).

My friends and I weren't big fighters. We were by no means hoodlums, the type of guys that go out on a given night itching for a brawl. We weren't, however, ones to back away from a fight either. If the cause was right, the opponent sufficiently loathsome, and sufficient alcohol was consumed, we were ready to hold our own.

This altercation is emblematic of a kind of by-product of a dynamic between disparate groups of high school males that creates a sort of natural animosity between the teenage clans. This dynamic usually presents in three different forms: academic, geographic, and cultural.

First, academically (I use the term loosely), there were the sports rivalries from the four other Yonkers city high schools. Lincoln High School, where by the way, a number of my cousins went, was a particularly detestable opponent whether it be on the court, the gridiron, or baseball diamond. This venom could easily be transferred from on the field to a tap room or a parking lot.

Second, geographically, there was the town of Eastchester, where we started to hang out from time to time toward the end of our high school tenures. They didn't like us "on their turf" or dating "their girls" and, as a rule at that time, we didn't like them. I can remember more than one "Oldies Night" at "The Place" when tables overturned and fisticuffs broke out.

Third, culturally, there was the variety of a-holes one might encounter on a given night at the discos of Mount Vernon or the rock and roll clubs of Yonkers and White Plains. For some reason, members of these diametrically opposed factions would, on occasion, feel emboldened to act like dicks and start trouble. However, as these two disparate groups would not be caught dead frequenting the same hot spots, these encounters would never happen at the same time or place.

New Rochelle, having an especially vibrant and diverse nightlife at the time, could produce the occasional donnybrook at a variety of musical genres, including, for example, Peachtree's (disco) or Glen Island Casino (rock and roll). The North Avenue bars were also fertile ground for these infrequent pugilistic engagements.

In any event, on this January night in 1980, we found ourselves in the middle of an altercation; however, this time there was clear and convincing justification for our actions. Some, probably Yonkers, Mount Vernon, or the Bronx dickweeds, were picking on a much smaller and weaker guy. With size, strength, and numbers on the side of the assholes, there was only one action to take on our part.

Like modern-day Knights of the Round Table, we joined the fray, intervening in order to protect and to save the honor (and probably the ass) of the smaller guy. At least that's how I'd like to look at it. The fight spilled out into the street. We kicked ass. With us that night by our side was a soon-to-be American hero who shall remain nameless.

Waking up the next day with a huge bump on the back of my left hand, I headed to the hospital for X-rays. Of course, I told my parents that my hand had gotten stepped on in a touch football game. And so I went back to Oneonta that semester with four pins holding my split fourth metacarpal together and a cast on my hand. I watched the Super Bowl at Tobey Hall in this condition.

So, why was I so confident about the game? Maybe it was the fact that the Rams, as they had shown throughout the decade, were simply not the Vikings or the Cowboys. Possibly, I had gotten so used to successes on the playing field that I had become immune to the thought that my teams could lose. Remember, the Yankees had won the World Series in the falls of 1977 and 1978, followed by the Steelers' victory over the Cowboys in January of 1979, and followed further by the Pirates' defeat of the Orioles in the 1979 fall classic. The Steel Curtain had gone 12-4 during the regular season and, again, rolled through the AFC playoffs.

Given this, I am afraid that I do not have as much to say about Super Bowl XIV as I did the other Pittsburgh championship rings. The main reason being I just wasn't sweating this game like the others.

For example, I was not worried at the end of the first quarter with the Rams holding a 7-3 lead. There was no discernible concern on my face when the two teams went into the locker room at halftime, Rams 13, Steelers 10. And, I did not freak out, pace the floor, or start cursing the gods after having taken the lead early in the third quarter, the Steel Curtain got fooled on a halfback option play by Lawrence McCutcheon, putting the Rams back up 19-17. Heading into the fourth quarter, I simply knew the Steelers were going to win.

And I was right. Less than three minutes into the final stanza, Terry Bradshaw's seventy-three-yard bomb to John Stallworth put the Steelers in the lead for good. For the rest of the game, about twelve minutes, the Steel Curtain rose up one last time and held the Rams to only seventy-five yards over three possessions, interrupting one of them with a Jack Lambert interception that, in turn, led to a four-minute Pittsburgh drive for the final touchdown of the game just after the two-minute warning. When it was over, the final score was Steelers 31, Rams 19. And I knew it all along.

Chapter 13
Requiem for an Idol

On June 26, 1979, Bobby Murcer returned from his National League exile after being traded back to New York from the Chicago Cubs. While there was some excitement for me about the event, the euphoria that I held for Murcer in the early '70s had waned. He was no longer the person I imitated while I was on the field. The Adirondack bat I used in high school playing first base for the Roosevelt Indians had no sponge taped to the handle. It now boasted a Reggie Jackson signature. The Murcer icon had been replaced by the Golden Calf that was Mr. October.

When Murcer returned to the hallowed ground of Yankee Stadium, things were markedly different. First, Murcer's stock had fallen considerably. While he had a better-than-average career with both the Giants and the Cubs, and was, at the time, the highest paid ballplayer in either team's history, when the Cubs traded Bobby back to New York, all they got in return was a minor league pitching prospect, Paul Semall.

"Paul, who?" you say. And you would be correct. After the Murcer trade, Semall ended up bouncing around the minor leagues in the employ of teams such as the Cubs and the Texas Rangers. His career ended in 1985 playing for the Hawaii Islanders, a AAA team in the Pirates organization.

During his tenure with the Giants, Murcer batted a total of .279, hit 25 home runs, and knocked in 181 RBIs. Over the two and a half years he played with the Cubs, he batted .270, hit 36 home runs, and drove in 153 runs. Not too shabby, but nowhere near the success he experienced, or what would have been expected of him had he remained in pinstripes. Plus, playing for teams like the Giants and the Cubs in the mid to late 70s was the equivalent of Napoleon's banishment, respectively, to Elba and Saint Helena. The Giants, over 1975–1976, finished a total of 55 and a half games out of first place in the NL West. The Cubs fared slightly better in the sense that just sucking is slightly better than being pathetic. The Cubs' divisional deficits from 1977 when Murcer arrived, until his departure in June of 1979, totaled 37 games out of the running.

Second, manager Billy Martin had taken the number "1" that Murcer used to wear. In his Yankees playing days, Martin had also sported *numero uno,* and he had reclaimed the number as his own when he was named Yankee Skipper in 1975.

Upon his return, Murcer was relegated to wearing number "2," a number that had yet to achieve retirement status as a result of the Derek Jeter era. Yes, number 2 had been worn by Yankees legends Red Rolfe and Frank Crosetti in the 1930s and '40s, both of whom I can recall my father making mention of when talking about the good old days when the subway was a nickel and movies cost a dime. Rolfe, Crosetti, and another number 2, George "Snuffy" Stirnweiss, played on teams that won a total of nine World Series, but, subsequently, the jersey number had fallen on hard times. More recently, during Murcer's playing time in New York and prior to his return, the number had been donned by fairly solid but mediocre players like Jerry Kenney, Sandy Alomar, and Matty Alou. In fact, at the time he was traded by the Cubs, Murcer's number 2 amounted to a mere hand-me-down from former Oriole, Paul Blair, who wore the uniform from 1977–1978, and was released by the Yankees at the beginning of the 1979 season.

Third, upon his return, the player that was once touted to be the next Mickey Mantle would now, at age 33, basically be relegated to a part-time player. By June of '79, Murcer was long removed from being one of the "Pride(s) of the New Yankees," as *Sports Illustrated* dubbed him back in 1973. Over the four and a half years after his return to the House That Ruth Built, Murcer, in 841 at bats, batted a mere .260, hit 35 home runs, and managed to drive in 145 runs. He was released by the Yankees on June 20, 1983, when, after only 23 plate appearances, he managed only 4 hits. The one RBI he tallied came as the result of his own foot touching home plate after hitting his one and only homer.

Lastly, and perhaps most painful for me, was the fact that Bobby had missed the three trips to the World Series and the two championships. He wasn't there for the Chambliss homer. He wasn't in the dugout when Reggie smashed three homers off the Dodgers in game six of the '77 series. He missed the Boston Massacre and the crushing of the hopes of Red Sox players and fans in the 1978 AL East tiebreaker game.

But baseball, more so than other sports, and life, provides opportunities for redemption. It has long been held by sports purists that the difficulty-to-success ratio associated with baseball (i.e., hitting the ball safely and getting on base three times out of ten over a career likely gets one into Cooperstown) makes baseball the most difficult of all sports.

To contrast, if an NFL quarterback averages a 30 percent completion percentage over his career, or, some NBA guard or forward consistently only hits three out of ten from the floor, they'd more likely be headed either to the bench, the showers, or early retirement rather than the Hall of Fame.

In baseball, however, you can stink up the joint for three at bats and come up in the bottom of the ninth, down one, with runners on second and third and lace a single to the opposite field or yank a curveball into the right field stands and become an instant hero. If the stakes are high enough, and the game important enough, you can promptly be etched in the annals of team lore. For a more detailed explanation, google "Bucky Dent and Boston Red Sox."

Bobby Murcer's redemption came on August 6, 1979, six weeks after being traded from the Cubs. Four days earlier, on August 2, tragedy struck the Yankees clubhouse. Murcer's early '70s Yankees compatriot and dear friend, Thurman Munson, died piloting his Cessna Citation aircraft while attempting a practice landing at Akron-Canton Regional Airport. Munson, beloved by the fans, and the first player to be named Yankees captain since Lou Gehrig, had been certified as a pilot about a year and a half prior to that fateful August afternoon. Over that time, he'd fly home to spend off days with his family. On August 1, the Yankees had just completed a three-game sweep of the White Sox at Comiskey Park. Munson took the short flight from Chicago to Canton to spend the evening and next day with his wife and three children.

The event shook the team to its core, especially Munson's closest friends, Lou Pinella and Murcer. On Friday, August 3, the Yankees started a four-game series with the Baltimore Orioles. The pregame ceremony included the Yankees taking the field and leaving the catcher's box eerily vacant. The rest of the team, as did the Orioles squad, lined up on the field in front of their dugouts, caps over hearts. Immediately thereafter came an impassioned prayer from Terence Cardinal Cooke, archbishop of the diocese of New York, and a stirring rendition of *God Bless America* by Robert Merrill. This was followed by an eight-minute long-standing ovation from the 51,151 faithful that were in attendance.

Despite a masterful two-hit performance by veteran pitcher Luis Tiant, the Yankees bats were flat and the Orioles won the game 1-0.

Notwithstanding the emotional weight that the game carried, and, in that moment, win-loss was not a high priority for both teams and fans, there was something disappointingly amiss about a loss on a day meant to honor the captain.

Simultaneously with the days around Munson's death, my friends and I had taken one of our patented road trips to Wildwood, New Jersey. In high school, Wildwood was our go-to place for drinking, cruising for girls, and general teenage idiocy. A few years later, the Hamptons would replace Wildwood as a summer party destination, although, personally, I never liked the place. Something about driving home on that nightmare that is the Long Island Expressway on a Sunday night. Therefore, I only went to the Hamptons once or twice. In any event, for us, in those days, Wildwood was, hands down, the Valhalla of rapturous tomfoolery.

Initially, my friend Murray and I had a hurdle to overcome before heading to the Jersey Shore. We worked in the frozen food department at the Pathmark supermarket on Central Avenue and were both scheduled to work the weekend. This may have seemed to be an insurmountable obstacle for more responsible teenagers with a conscience, but not for us.

In the silver-tongued style of high schoolers motivated by an event that, as with many frivolous escapades during adolescence, was a life-or-death situation, we mapped out a plan. With the sincerity of truants swearing to the principal never again to cut school, we managed to get the frozen food manager to allow us to work the overnight shift and get all of our work done so we could leave for Wildwood in the morning.

Our manager, Zach, was an affable guy. He was always cool with us when it came to work. I think we probably reminded him of his own youth, as he welcomed conversations about our exploits with alcohol, women, or the occasional fistfight and was more than happy to relay his own experiences. Assuming he wasn't a person afflicted with chronic conjunctivitis, we often observed that Zach liked to get high. Perhaps this contributed to his affability and accommodating nature. In fact, we kind of viewed him as an old hippie, although it was likely he was only in his late twenties or early thirties. To a high schooler, most adults, especially those in dubious positions of authority, appear ancient. However, if Zach had denied our request to implement our overnight work scheme, there was a good possibility we'd end up quitting. My friends and I had quit other jobs for less, like for a touch football game that "desperately needed one more guy."

Of course we rewarded Zach's magnanimity in the typical way high school kids revved up for a trip to the Jersey Shore would have. We moved the scores of boxes of frozen Gorton's fish filets, Green Giant vegetables, Breyers ice cream, and Tree Tavern pizzas from their pallets to a U-boat and hid them in the back of the walk-in box.

We had heard the news of Munson's death and spoke about it on our trip down to the shore. As die-hard Yankees fans, we all loved Munson and the news jolted us emotionally, at least as much as teenage boys could be emotional back in the day. But the question of what the Yankees would be without Munson, after so many years, was also on the minds. No one took it harder than another of my best friends, Moose. Munson was to him what Bobby Murcer had been to me.

I do not remember much from the weekend in Wildwood. In fact, I had to be reminded for this book by my friends of many of the comings and goings from that weekend. The really big news was that one of my friends lost his virginity with a gal, we think, was from South Philly. Or, was it Montreal? Apparently, I was with her friend, but the tryst ended in nothing more than a make-out session. This may explain my friend's lucidity and my opacity about the events of that evening.

Somewhere along the way, perhaps as late as the return trip, we heard that Munson's funeral would be on Monday, August 6, and the fourth game of the series against the Orioles would go on as scheduled. Whether one of us came up with the idea of attending the Monday night game, or it was one of those spontaneous bursts of brilliance that resembles the collision of protons in the Large Hadron Collider, we decided to head to the Bronx on Monday for the Oriole game. At any rate, having missed the Friday tribute game, the Wildwood crew felt compelled to extend the vacation one more day and pay homage to the Yankees captain. It was the least we could do.

Much like the Wildwood trip, I do not remember much about the early part of the game that was carried nationally on ABC with Howard Cosell, Keith Jackson, and Dodger legend Don Drysdale in the booth. From our seats in the upper deck down the third base line, there was certainly a feeling of somberness, both seriousness and sadness, hanging over the stadium. This aura also enveloped the team throughout the game, despite some periodic prompting from the fans. As the Yankees took the field, like Friday night, the catcher's box was left empty for a few moments, again highlighting Munson's absence.

For much of the night, the Yankees were as flat as they were on Friday, the day after Munson's death. This time, however, along with the bats, the pitching was failing them as well. Yankees ace Ron Guidry was giving a mediocre performance by his standards. Guidry had given up eight hits over seven innings, including a home run to the Orioles' Ken Singleton. Baltimore built up a 4-0 lead and was poised to once again spoil a night set aside for honoring the fallen Yankees captain.

In contrast, Oriole pitcher Dennis Martinez, who came into the game with a 14-8 record had stopped the Yankees cold all night, scattering just four hits over six and two-thirds innings.

The Orioles went down in the top of the seventh and the crowd stood per baseball game decorum. I can't remember whether or not the fans began to cheer or attempted to awaken the team from their pedestrian slumber during the seventh-inning stretch. If there was an effort to revive the team, it appeared to dissipate quickly as outfielder Bobby Brown and Munson replacement Brad Gulden made two quick outs on only three pitches to start the inning.

Then, something happened. No one saw it, heard it, or even knew it had happened, but it did. Martinez, who had been virtually unhittable to this point, suddenly, inexplicably, lost it. In the parlance of athletic contests, the wheels had come off completely for Martinez. Romantically, spiritually, cosmically, however you want to put it, the series of events over the next two innings belongs in the annals of Major League Baseball history as much as Bobby Thompson's or Kirk Gibson's home runs, Willie Mays's catch, Mookie Wilson's grounder. Or at least that's how I see it.

Looking back, I'd like to think Thurman was behind this. Leaving the cemetery in Canton, Ohio, he made a detour by way of the Bronx on his ascent toward the Pearly Gates and took one last pass over Yankee Stadium before his eternal rest.

With two out and no one on, the next batter, the 0-for-2 Bucky Dent, drew a walk on four pitches. Willie Randolph, who had one of the four Yankees hits off of Martinez, ripped a 2-1 curveball into the left field corner for a double, moving Dent to third with two outs.

What happened next was surreal, a thing of legend and fantasy and folklore. Bobby Murcer walked to the plate. The same Bobby Murcer that had delivered one of the two eulogies at his good friend's funeral only hours before. As I would see after reviewing the game online years later, the ABC broadcast put up two graphics when Murcer stepped in the batter's box. One, Murcer had been 0-for-3 on the night. Second, since his return to New York, he had been 0 for 15 with two outs and runners on base.

It can be said that all professional sports are rooted as much in superstition as they are talent and skill. Like a football announcer saying that a kicker hasn't missed an extra point all year before the boot is shanked, the Murcer statistical information was going to lead to something. Whether the pox would fall on Murcer's or Martinez's house remained to be seen. In any event, the malocchio was about to be put on someone.

But the fans in the stadium weren't watching the ABC feed, and Randolph's double had gotten the crowd back in the game and given everyone new life.

Many at the game my age, slightly younger, or certainly older knew who was at the plate and what he had done so many times years before. Suddenly, fifty-one-thousand-plus fans were transported back to 1973. Murcer turned on a 1-1 pitch from Martinez and sent a frozen rope into the lower deck in right field. The score was now 4-3 and the crowd went berserk, including me and the boys. It was the type of emotional explosion that is unique to sporting events, where perfect strangers hug and give each other high fives.

The Yankees still trailed by a run, however, and while Shakespeare never wrote about baseball, he certainly could have penned the final act this night.

With neither team scoring over the next inning and a half, the stage was set for a dramatic bottom of the ninth. As it turned out, the same group that had provided the excitement in the bottom of the seventh was up, in the on-deck circle, and standing on the top step of the dugout. There was also still a Martinez on the mound, but Dennis had been sent to the showers and Tippy had taken the mound after the Murcer home run. Tippy Martinez was a formidable reliever, posting a 10-3 record backed up by ten saves in 1979.

Leading off, Bucky Dent drew a walk as he did in the seventh. Willie Randolph, who had doubled in the seventh, was given the bunt sign. Randolph squared and poked the pitch toward first, in between Martinez and charging first baseman Eddie Murray. Inexplicably, the Orioles reliever picked up the ball and threw it wildly to first, sending the ball into right field. Dent moved to third on the play and Randolph to second.

So, as it was two innings prior, Bobby Murcer walked into the batter's box with the same two runners set in scoring position. Two things differed, however. This time, Murcer came to the plate with nobody out, not two, like the seventh.

Second, the Yanks were now down by one, not four, as was the case when he blasted his three-run shot. All that the Bronx Bombers needed was a base hit to secure not only a tie score but the win.

Murcer, perhaps pumping with adrenaline and anticipation, quickly got behind on the count 0-2. If the homer in the seventh was surreal, what happened next could only be described as paranormal. Martinez delivered the pitch on the outside of the plate, standard operating procedure with a two-strike count (i.e., don't give the batter anything good to hit). Murcer, the career dead pull hitter, went the other way, lacing the ball into the left field corner and scoring both Dent and Randolph. If Murcer's seventh-inning exploits had whipped the crowd into a frenzy, his-ninth inning heroics brought bedlam to the Bronx. More hugs and high fives were exchanged among friends and strangers.

On the day they buried their captain, the Yankees had pulled off a miracle. A miracle engineered single handedly by Bobby Murcer. And we were there.

As an odd but interesting aside, while the Orioles cakewalked to the AL pennant that year, it would be in spite of, rather than due to, Dennis Martinez. After the August 6 debacle, Martinez went 1-8 down the stretch, finishing the season with fifteen wins against sixteen losses. I guess we know who got the malocchio.

Murcer was with the team for the 1980 World Series loss to the Dodgers, but he only had three plate appearances and went hitless.

Bobby Murcer, fittingly, was the last active player to have been a teammate of Mickey Mantle. He was also the only Yankee to play alongside the likes of Mantle, Ford, Munson, Howard, Maris, Reggie, Mattingly, and Guidry.

His final game came on June 11, 1983. On August 7, 1983, the Yankees honored his years in pinstripes with "Bobby Murcer Day."

After his Yankees retirement, Bobby turned in his cleats for a microphone and moved directly into the broadcast booth. He would spend the next twenty-five years there, working for WPIX, WYNY, and the YES Network. He punctuated this time working for the Yankees as a coach and in the front office.

In late 2006, Murcer was diagnosed with a brain tumor. Shortly thereafter, it was announced that the tumor was malignant. Bobby Ray Murcer died on July 12, 2008, after a prolonged battle with brain cancer. He was sixty-two.

Just prior to his death, in May 2008, Murcer's autobiography, *Yankee for Life: My 40-Year Journey in Pinstripes,* was published. It covers the pressure of being the "next Mickey Mantle" and his disappointment at being traded. In the 304-page book, Murcer spends a little over four pages recounting Munson's death and the days surrounding it. However, when it came to his heroics in the Monday night game against the Orioles, the humble Yankee took only twenty-seven words to describe that historic moment: "In the seventh, I hit a three-run homer to make it 4-3. Then, in the bottom of the ninth, I hit a two-run single. Yankees win, 5-4."

It took me over two thousand words to do it justice.

Epilogue

On Friday, February 22, 1980, most of the Oneonta student body had vacated campus and taken off for home. At the end of classes that day, a ten day, I believe referred to as the midwinter recess, ensued and classes would not recommence until Monday, March 3. Typically, the only poor schlubs that got stuck taking Friday classes were freshmen, and by second semester, even many of them had gotten the knack of avoiding end-of-week classes, especially given the vibrant Thursday night bar scene in downtown Oneonta. In any event, everyone, but for a handful of us, was gone.

One thing was for sure: we weren't sticking around for a Friday night study session or some extra credit project. Two nights earlier, the US Olympic men's hockey team defeated West Germany, setting up a medal round contest against the Soviet Union on Friday night at 5:00 p.m.

Due to time differences between the two countries, attempts at moving the game to prime time for a bigger American audience went for naught as the Soviets didn't want the nomenklatura in Moscow to have to watch the game at 4:00 a.m. I guess one o'clock in the morning was just swell. The move, however, would have allowed the people of Yakutsk,

Siberia, to see the game at 10:00 a.m., but the Russians never cared much for Siberia, unless, that is, they were sending a dissident poet there.

In any event, the 5:00 p.m. puck drop meant that ABC, who was televising the Olympic games, would have to show the game on tape delay at 8:00 p.m. EST in order to maximize the national audience.

Without going into a dissertation on Cold War relations, suffice it to say that, from a sports perspective, the Soviet hockey team was hated as much as any rival in any sport. For many people in the seventies, the geopolitical struggle between the US and its NATO (North Atlantic Treaty Organization) allies and the Soviet Bloc was played out, not in the situation room but on the basketball court, the balance beam, the boxing ring, and the hockey rink. In this context, for me, the Russians were the Cowboys, Raiders, Reds, and Red Sox, all rolled into one.

The Soviet hockey team had dominated every Winter Olympic games since my existence on this earth. They won gold at Innsbruck twice, in 1964 and 1976; at Grenoble in 1968; and in Sapporo in 1972 and were the overwhelming favorites heading into Lake Placid in 1980. In addition, they were known as the Red Army team, a lame attempt to give the impression that these guys were simple military conscripts, who just skated well and wanted to represent Mother Russia on the ice. Hypocritically, they did not, however, join their comrades when the Soviets invaded Afghanistan in December of 1979. The truth was the Soviet hockey players were in the army like Elvis was "in the army." As if the King of Rock and Roll, who was assigned to an armored tank division in Germany, could have, if only he were around at the time, accompanied Patton as he slashed his way through the Ardennes in 1944. During those days, all American athletes were amateurs. The Soviets were professionals, and everyone knew it. They not only wanted world domination, but they were cheaters too.

The bus ride from Oneonta to White Plains, where the Trailways terminal was an arduous one, took about six hours. Almost twice as much as the car ride. With the added trip home to Yonkers, I'd be pushing the issue for being able to catch the game. It would've been at least another hour for the Long Island kids. Plus, during the ride, some jerk might blurt out the score and ruin things as the game would likely already be underway. So a group of us decided to stay in the dorm for the game and postpone that miserable bus trek home for a day.

I couldn't tell you how many of us stayed. I only remember one person, Stu Reinfeld, who was a friend of Eddie Young and one of the juniors that made our freshman year dorm life more palatable. Those of us that stayed behind that evening were sworn to silence. Under penalty of death, a strict radio and television silence was put into effect.

The game that became known as the "Miracle on Ice" has been well documented over the years. Every tenth year anniversary, and there have now been four, opens up the floodgates of television and print (and now online) retrospectives. Also, there are the two film adaptations. One, the more recent Disney version, is an utterly enjoyable flick with Kurt Russell playing the dispassionate but greatly respected taskmaster, head coach Herb Brooks. The other is a 1981 made-for-TV movie starring, of all people, Karl Malden wearing a bad wig as Brooks, and Jessica Walter, often cast as the sultry temptress, playing Brooks's demure wife, Patti.

In any event, an in-depth, blow-by-blow play-by-play of that historical contest is not necessary. Everyone knows what happened. The Soviets and the Americans traded goals throughout the game. Briefly:

First period:

9:12, USSR 1, USA 0,

14:03, USSR 1, USA 1,

17:34, USSR 2, USA 1,

19:59, USSR 2, USA 2.

Second period:

17:42, USSR 3, USA 2.

Third period:
8:39, USSR 3, USA 3,
10:00, USA 4, USSR 3.

What stands out about that game, besides sending the USSR home with their tails between their legs, was the level of psychological exhaustion it took to watch the contest as a sports fan. Despite all of the trials, tribulations, and achievements I had experienced with Pirates, Steelers, and Yankees teams over the past decade, none were as exciting, exhilarating, and suspenseful as that hockey game. I cannot remember any other sporting event of the decade, perhaps ever, that brought with it such an emotional roller coaster for such a sustained amount of time.

Throughout the contest, we were all waiting for a shoe to drop, a shoe in the form of a big Soviet skate. I was terrified that the US would lose. I would have been emotionally devastated if we did; yet, at some level it seemed almost inevitable. I think deep down, we felt as though the fantasy would not be fulfilled.

Sixty minutes of regulation hockey turned into more than two hours of anticipation and stress. I was a wreck throughout most of the game. When the US scored, I was relieved not confident. Nowhere was this more apparent when Mike Eruzione netted the go-ahead goal, a moment of brief euphoria that occurred ten minutes into the third period. What Eruzione's heroics actually meant was that the US would have to hold the Soviets, winners of the last four Olympic gold medals and the best team in the world, at bay for a full ten minutes.

This constant fear of a Soviet comeback was, I believe, why Al Michaels could not begin to utter his most celebrated phrase, "Do you believe in miracles? Yes!" until there were only five seconds left in the game. Right up until that point, the Russians were more than capable of scoring.

The game was so emotionally exhausting that the rest of the US hockey team's run to the gold was anticlimactic, almost uninteresting. I think I treated the gold medal game against Finland much like the Steelers-Rams Super Bowl. To me it was never in doubt. Plus, it almost didn't matter. After the win over the USSR, the proverbial air had been taken out of the Olympic balloon.

◆◆◆

Following the Miracle on Ice, things changed in a way that brought an abrupt end for my 1970s sports experience. The 1980s arrived and major changes ensued, especially for my teams that enjoyed so much success during the prior ten years. The franchises that had provided so much excitement and joy would all but disappear from the landscape and virtually vanish from the postseason in the eighties. These would be barren days indeed.

This includes the Yanks suffering back-to-back revenge losses via a three-game ALCS sweep by the Royals in 1980, and a four-games-to-two World Series loss to the Dodgers in the strike-shortened 1981 season. Despite a successful formula in the '70s, George Steinbrenner's obsession with free agency became manic and led to high payrolls, disappointing results, and a revolving door of managerial changes with Billy Martin caught in the rotator. The Bronx Bombers would not return to the fall classic until their epic run of 1996, 1998, 1999, 2000, 2001, 2003, and 2009.

The Pirates, on the other hand, forgot how to play baseball completely. The Bucs spent most of the decade near or in the NL East cellar, before climbing out and losing three heartbreaking NLCS series in the early 1990s—two to the Braves and, once again, to the fucking Reds.

The Steelers would sniff around the playoffs here and there, but even an appearance in the 1984 AFC championship game against the

Dolphins seemed like a prekickoff fait accompli. Dolphins 45, Steelers 28.

During the 1980s Pittsburgh would be outplayed and surpassed by their divisional rivals and former 1970s doormats, the Bengals and Browns. Despite rooting for them against the hated 49ers, Cincinnati fell short in both of its eighties Super Bowl appearances. The Browns, perpetually tragic, lost back-to-back AFC championship heartbreakers against the Broncos in 1986 and 1987 and never made it to a Super Bowl. In fact, with the exception of two Raiders Super Bowls, the entire AFC, in general, forgot how to play defense during the Forgettable Decade. Conversely, the Steelers, who always had a respectable D, forgot how to play offense.

As for the Steelers, their run of three Super Bowl appearances between 2005 and 2010 is the only thing that might resemble a dynasty. But a 2010 lackluster performance and loss to the Packers in Super Bowl XLV, and the seemingly endless devastations of losing AFC championship and playoff games to the Patriots, have put to bed any comparisons to the Steel Curtain of the 1970s.

In the end, despite all of my bitching and moaning about teams like the Reds, Orioles, Raiders, and Cowboys, as it turned out, maybe I really don't have too much to complain about.

Although the Reds won two World Series in the 1970s, they lost two as well. The Orioles appeared three times in the fall classic and lost twice. The Raiders, despite appearing in five AFC championship games, walked away with only one Forgettable Decade Lombardi Trophy. Dallas won two Super Bowls, but lost three. And God help the valiant Vikings fans, including one of my best friends, Willie, who had to sit through four Super Bowl losses.

As I get older, I am reinforced in the premise of the book, that the 1970s—my seventies—were the greatest decade experienced by any fan, ever. I suppose fans, past and present, will have their own lists to challenge the assertion, but I still believe mine is unmatched for the concentration of success in such a compressed period of time.

Furthermore, I am confident in my proclamation as, fifty years removed from these events, I can say things from that vaunted era that less and less people that are around these days can say:

I watched the Immaculate Reception, live;

I witnessed Chambliss's home run, in person;

I was at the Munson memorial game;

I saw Clemente play.

In first-year law school torts class, we were introduced to a legal concept that reinforces the precept of this book, *res ipsa loquitur*, "the thing speaks for itself."

Moving forward, despite subsequent years where, from time to time, my teams have led me to experience my own seasons of malaise, I am not deterred. To conclude here where we began, with another quote by Dickens, "I wear the chain I forged in life." Yes, it is a ponderous chain, but I am stuck with the Pirates, Yankees, and Steelers. And I'm just fine with that.

Acknowledgments and Notes

For the writing and completion of this book, thanks must be given, first and foremost, to family and friends who lent their time and memories for filling in gaps and contributing to some of the persons, places, and events that are chronicled here.

Special thanks are also in order to Tim Breslin from the Detre Library & Archives at the Senator John Heinz History Center in Pittsburgh for clarifying things with respect to Babushka Night.

Also, kudos to Sophia Dunne of the Archives & Special Collections team at the Milne Library at SUNY Oneonta for helping me find information surrounding some of the key dates for the 1979–1980 academic calendar.

Where memory failed me and statistics, trade, play-by-play, and other player information was necessary, websites such as Baseball-Reference.com, Baseball-Almanac.com, and Pro-Football-Reference.com proved invaluable.

In an effort to protect the innocent, as well as the not so innocent, the names of the individuals referenced in this book are those of real people, unless they are made up.

About the Author

Jim Bellano, an avid sports enthusiast and passionate devotee of all things 1970s, has penned a delightful memoir that encapsulates the thrill of that era's sports scene. With a keen sense of humor and an eye for vivid storytelling, Bellano invites readers on an entertaining journey through his teenage years in New York and Pennsylvania. Beyond his passion for sports, Bellano has spent his professional career as an attorney, an economic development professional, an adjunct professor and an author of numerous opinion pieces. Now, he brings his unique blend of wit and wisdom to the pages of *Fond Memories From the Forgettable Decade.*